NAMEPLATES OF THE BIG FOUR INCLUDING BRITISH RAILWAYS

Driver Alfred Hurley and Fireman James Lester admire the nameplate and coat of arms of Bulleid Pacific No.34051 whilst it was being prepared for the funeral train of Sir Winston Churchill on January 30th, 1965.

Fox Photos

NAMEPLATES
OF THE BIG FOUR
INCLUDING BRITISH RAILWAYS

FRANK BURRIDGE

Oxford Publishing Co.

© 1975 Frank Burridge and Oxford Publishing Co.

Reprinted 1985

ISBN 0 902888 43 9

Printed in Great Britain
by Netherwood Dalton & Co. Ltd, Huddersfield, Yorks.

Published by
Oxford Publishing Co.
Link House
West Street
POOLE, Dorset

INTRODUCTION

The locomotives have gone, but their nameplates linger on! There was always something special about a locomotive that carried a name, yet, little did I think when compiling *The Nameplate Series* of booklets after the war, that such an interest would still be alive today.

Neither did British Railways, for when they dispensed with their steam locomotives, they sold off the nameplates at virtually scrap-metal prices! Buying one of those brass plates now, would cost you well into three figures, that's assuming you were lucky enough to be offered one! Most of them are kept in private collections hidden away from public view, so *this book is dedicated to all those enthusiasts who would dearly like to see some of them again, if only in print.*

Basically, this is a pictorial review. I have not attempted to go into elaborate details regarding the origins of the names, or indeed, catalogue the early types. What I have tried to do here is to concentrate on those plates fitted by the Four Main railways since 1923, together with the final ones introduced by British Railways.

For easy reference, the Big Four appear in numerical order as allocated by British Railways,

and these numbers are quoted throughout as they were the final ones at the time of scrapping. However, each class within its section appears, more or less, in the order it was named.

Grateful thanks are extended to all those who so happily contributed their treasured pictures. Many thousands were examined so as to show the best possible detail. Modellers will doubtless appreciate the drawings also included.

Incidentally, because the original blueprints were not always adhered to exactly, most of the measurements given were taken from the actual nameplates. Thanks this time to all those private collectors who allowed me to use my tape measure.

For the first time in any book, the names have been printed, as near as possible, in the style they appeared on the locomotives. In this respect, great efforts have been made by numerous friends particularly Keith Buckle, Frank Davis, Wallie Eccles and Brian Hilton, to ensure that they are accurate. My son, Russell, also helped with many details. As for my part, it has been fascinating to relive those adolescent days, selecting and arranging the many illustrations into what I hope will become a standard work of reference.

Frank Burridge

One of the earliest known examples of a nameplate, and being fitted to the wheels, probably the most unique. This 0-4-0 locomotive was built for the Shutt End Colliery Railway, Kingswinford, Staffs. It is now preserved.

D. Eatwell

CONTENTS

NOTES
- The lists of names, and those quoted in captions, have been type set in CAPITALS as used for the nameplates, and where the size of the letters also differ, as with the S.R. 'Merchant Navy' class for example, the names have been adjusted, approximately to the comparative size.

- The measurements on the drawings throughout, unless stated, are taken from the face of the nameplates. Slight variations may be found with other plates of the same class due to trimming after casting, or the degree to which they were polished during and after service!

- Some nameplates may have appeared in service before the dates of the official naming ceremonies.

- Where a locomotive was renamed before receiving its final B.R. number, as shown, its previous number would apply to the original name.

IN THE BEGINNING

Unlike the other three main companies formed in 1923, the G.W.R. dated back to 1835. It started life as the 7ft. 0¼in. broad gauge, but eventually, the whole system was converted to the standard 4ft. 8½in. gauge.

Above right: One of the four broad gauge locomotives delivered in November, 1837 by R. Stephenson & Co. NORTH STAR had its nameplates divided into two sections each side of the axle-box.

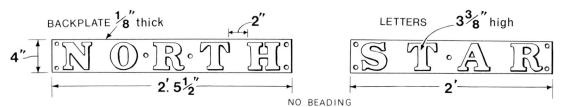

VULCAN was actually the first to run on the G.W.R. on December 28th, 1837. Built by Tayleur & Co., it had solid cast nameplates, as did some of the earlier locomotives of the line.

Another example, this time curved. HAWK, one of the 2-4-0 'Hawthorn' Class, was built at Swindon in December, 1865.

Built at Swindon in March 1851, LORD OF THE ISLES had its nameplates fitted just above the centre of the wheels. The Royal Arms were displayed for State visits. *British Rail Photos*

This standard gauge version, built in January, 1895, had nameplates with much bolder letters and more curvature.

8

Left: No.471 SIR WATKIN, built in 1869, was one of the few G.W.R locomotives which had the lettering recessed into a brass plate and originally wax-filled, similar to the L.N.W.R. nameplates. *Ian Allan Library*

CHARLES SAUNDERS *above* and ARMSTRONG *below left*, both built in 1894, had nameplates without brass beading. *British Rail*

Built in 1883 and named in 1896, FAIR ROSAMUND was one of the few tank engines to be named by the G.W.R. It survived until 1935.

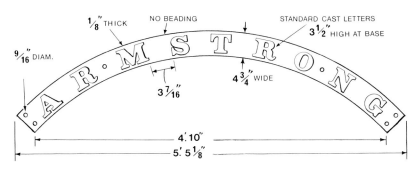

Eventually G.W.R. nameplates were framed with brass beading and this one was fitted on the boiler, clear of the wheel splasher. *British Rail*

1895 saw the introduction of the 'Duke' class, and a number of them were given straight nameplates fitted to the boiler. These were exchanged for the standard curved pattern from 1903. *British Rail*

Originally named LIZARD, the above 'Duke' class locomotive was renamed THE LIZARD in 1904. *L. Hanson*

BULLDOG was built in 1898 as a 'Duke' with straight nameplates *as above*, but in 1905 these were replaced by curved ones fitted to the wheel splashers. *British Rail*

Originally one of the 'Camel' class, BULLDOG was rebuilt as a '3300' class locomotive in 1906. Forty-one others in the class however, had oval nameplates *as below*. *Ian Allan Library*

Seven of the oval 'Bulldog' plates had the Great Western coat of arms displayed in the centre.

All but a few of these plates had the building dates removed during service, to disguise that they were veteran engines! *F.B.*

Odd man out! WATERFORD a 'Badminton' class locomotive had the distinction of having standard letters with a works plate in the centre. *Real Photos*

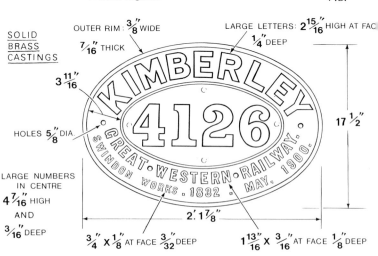

The above was one of the 'Atbara' class to have combined name and number plates. Most of the measurements also apply to the other oval plates.

1900 onwards. The G.W.R. absorbed a number of tank engines which carried nameplates of the typical industrial pattern. The one above originally belonged to the Liskeard and Looe Railway.
Real Photos

1901 brought the introduction of two pannier tanks fitted with cranes and a third in 1921, all of which had straight nameplates.
British Rail

THE COUNTESS was one of two engines built in 1902 for the Welshpool and Llanfair Light Railway. After absorption, the nameplate was moved to the side of the cab, and because it did not fit, the 'THE' was cut-off!
Photomatic

1902 saw the first of the 'Saint' class. BIBURY COURT, built later, shows the typical way the brass letters were spaced out. The rivets showing on the splashers were a feature of the 'Saints' and some other locomotives of the period.
R.C. Riley

Right: In 1903 the first of the famous 'City' class appeared, and the nameplates were displayed in a similar fashion to the earlier 'Bulldog' class with the outside springs. The size of the small letters 'OF' is $2\frac{3}{8}$in. high by $\frac{3}{8}$in. wide at the face.
J. Oatway

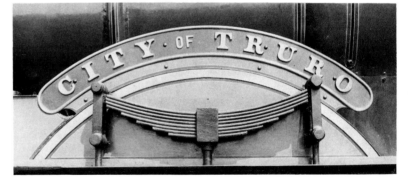

1903 saw the importation of a French Atlantic with its own plate fitted to the cabside. Two more followed in 1905 and these had G.W.R. curved plates fitted to the splashers in 1907.

From 1904, the 4-4-0 'County' class came into being.

Curved plates were also fitted to the 4-6-0 'Star' class introduced in 1907. The splashers originally had brass beading and workplates, *as on the right.*

Built in 1908, No.111 was the Great Western's only Pacific locomotive. It was rebuilt in 1924 as a 'Castle' and renamed.
British Rail Photos

THE CONSTRUCTION OF G.W.R. NAMEPLATES

From the very beginning, the Great Western Railway adopted the use of bold serif lettering for its nameplates. There were a few exceptions to the rule as outlined in the previous pages, but since 1900, at any rate, the sole choice has been the rather chubby version of Clarendon Bold, the printing type face. These hollow-cast brass letters were $3\frac{1}{2}$ in. high at the base tapering to $3\frac{3}{8}$ in. at the face. Being $\frac{7}{16}$ in. thick, they were rivetted to sheet-steel plates, and here again, there was a certain amount of standardization. Quite often, long names had the letters almost touching each other, whilst shorter names had them spaced out, but not as much as on the earlier G.W.R. nameplates.

The ends of their nameplates were rounded because this suited the brass beading that was fitted to the edge of the back-plate, thus providing a frame for the lettering. The background between the polished letters and beading was black, with the lower portion in G.W.R. colours.

The curved nameplates were then fitted to the wheel splashers by means of three or four angle brackets of $\frac{1}{2}$ in. gauge steel. The accompanying drawings give further details, and below are illustrations of additions that appeared on some nameplates.

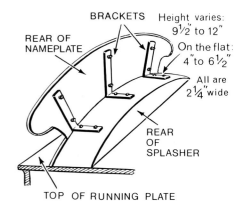

BRACKETS Height varies: $9\frac{1}{2}$" to 12"

REAR OF NAMEPLATE

On the flat: 4" to $6\frac{1}{2}$"

All are $2\frac{1}{4}$" wide

REAR OF SPLASHER

TOP OF RUNNING PLATE

'Saint' class No.2980 CŒUR DE LION. Width of diphthong: $5\frac{3}{8}$ in.
F.B.

'Star' class No.4017 KNIGHT OF LIÉGE, showing the *Acute* accent.
Real Photos

'Castle' class No.5064 BISHOP'S CASTLE. Width of apostrophe: $\frac{7}{8}$ in. Height: $1\frac{1}{2}$ in. Most others had a smaller apostrophe.
F.B.

'Hall' class No.6997 BRYN-IVOR HALL. Hyphen: $2\frac{1}{2}$ in. x $\frac{7}{16}$ in.
K. Leech

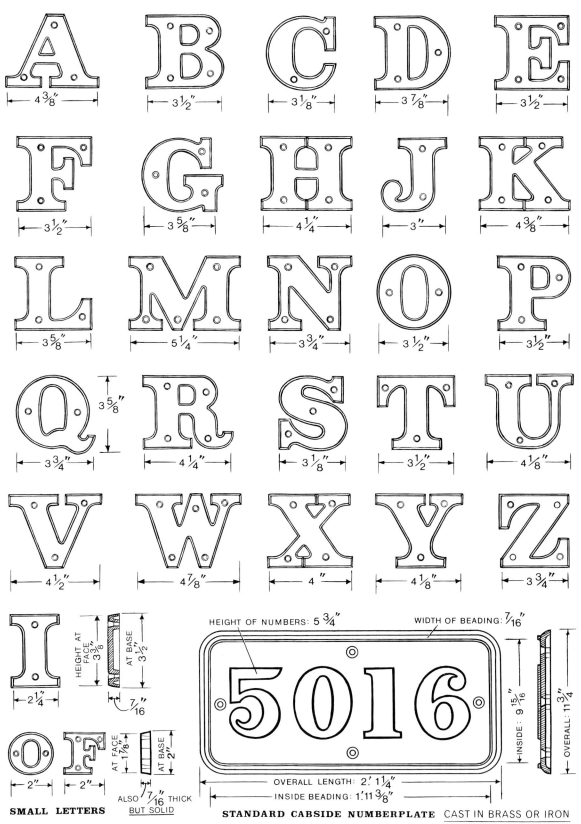

All the above letter widths were taken from the FACE of the castings and even these can vary up to $\frac{1}{16}$ in.
In view of the casting bevel an extra $\frac{1}{8}$ in. should be added to obtain the overall base measurements.

13

Above: As originally built, No.4074 CALDICOTT CASTLE was very soon renamed with only one 'T'. *British Rail*

'CASTLE' CLASS

The first 'Castle', No. 4073 was completed in August 192
Being a development of the earlier 'Star' class, a number
these were later rebuilt as 'Castles' starting in 1925.

Below: No.5016 MONTGOMERY CASTLE in its final form with double chimney and straight-sided tender. *R.O. Coffin*

G.O.P. Pearce

All the 'Castle' class nameplates were fitted above the centre wheel splashers. Here we see No.4082 which was often used for the Royal Train. In February, 1952, the number and nameplates were exchanged with those of No.7013 BRISTOL CASTLE.

On the right is one of the commemorative plates which were fitted to the cabsides. They measured $9\frac{1}{2}$in. wide by $6\frac{3}{8}$in. deep.

G R

THIS ENGINE
Nº 4082 WINDSOR CASTLE WAS BUILT AT
SWINDON IN APRIL 1924
AND WAS DRIVEN FROM THE WORKS TO THE STATION BY
HIS MAJESTY KING GEORGE V
ACCOMPANIED BY QUEEN MARY
ON THE OCCASION OF THE VISIT OF THEIR MAJESTIES
TO THE GREAT WESTERN RAILWAY WORKS AT
SWINDON ON APRIL 28ᵀᴴ 1924.

WITH THEIR MAJESTIES ON THE FOOTPLATE WERE
VISCOUNT CHURCHILL.	CHAIRMAN.
SIR FELIX POLE.	GENERAL MANAGER.
Mʳ C B.COLLETT.	CHIEF MECHANICAL ENGINEER.
LOCOMOTIVE INSPECTOR.	C.H.FLEWELLEN.
ENGINE DRIVER.	E R.B.ROWE.
FIREMAN.	A.W.COOK.

15

NUMBERS AND NAMES / INCLUDING THOSE SUBSEQUENTLY CARRIED

111 VISCOUNT CHURCHILL	
4000 NORTH STAR	
4009 SHOOTING STAR/	
100 A1 LLOYD'S	
4016 KNIGHT OF THE GOLDEN FLEECE/	
THE SOMERSET	
LIGHT INFANTRY	
(PRINCE ALBERT'S) *	

111 VISCOUNT CHURCHILL
4000 NORTH STAR
4009 SHOOTING STAR/
100 A1 LLOYD'S
4016 KNIGHT OF THE GOLDEN FLEECE/
    THE SOMERSET
    LIGHT INFANTRY
    (PRINCE ALBERT'S) *
4032 QUEEN ALEXANDRA
4037 QUEEN PHILIPPA/THE
    SOUTH WALES BORDERERS*
4073 CAERPHILLY CASTLE
4074 CALDICOTT CASTLE/
    CALDICOT CASTLE
4075 CARDIFF CASTLE
4076 CARMARTHEN CASTLE
4077 CHEPSTOW CASTLE
4078 PEMBROKE CASTLE
4079 PENDENNIS CASTLE
4080 POWDERHAM CASTLE
4081 WARWICK CASTLE
4082 WINDSOR CASTLE
4083 ABBOTSBURY CASTLE
4084 ABERYSTWYTH CASTLE
4085 BERKELEY CASTLE
4086 BUILTH CASTLE
4087 CARDIGAN CASTLE
4088 DARTMOUTH CASTLE
4089 DONNINGTON CASTLE
4090 DORCHESTER CASTLE
4091 DUDLEY CASTLE
4092 DUNRAVEN CASTLE
4093 DUNSTER CASTLE
4094 DYNEVOR CASTLE
4095 HARLECH CASTLE
4096 HIGHCLERE CASTLE
4097 KENILWORTH CASTLE
4098 KIDWELLY CASTLE
4099 KILGERRAN CASTLE
5000 LAUNCESTON CASTLE
5001 LLANDOVERY CASTLE
5002 LUDLOW CASTLE
5003 LULWORTH CASTLE
5004 LLANSTEPHAN CASTLE
5005 MANORBIER CASTLE
5006 TREGENNA CASTLE
5007 ROUGEMONT CASTLE
5008 RAGLAN CASTLE
5009 SHREWSBURY CASTLE
5010 RESTORMEL CASTLE
5011 TINTAGEL CASTLE
5012 BERRY POMEROY CASTLE
5013 ABERGAVENNY CASTLE
5014 GOODRICH CASTLE
5015 KINGSWEAR CASTLE
5016 MONTGOMERY CASTLE
5017 ST DONATS CASTLE/
    THE GLOUCESTERSHIRE
    REGIMENT 28TH 61ST *
5018 ST MAWES CASTLE
5019 TREAGO CASTLE
5020 TREMATON CASTLE
5021 WHITTINGTON CASTLE
5022 WIGMORE CASTLE
5023 BRECON CASTLE
5024 CAREW CASTLE
5025 CHIRK CASTLE
5026 CRICCIETH CASTLE
5027 FARLEIGH CASTLE
5028 LLANTILIO CASTLE
5029 NUNNEY CASTLE
5030 SHIRBURN CASTLE

5031 TOTNES CASTLE
5032 USK CASTLE
5033 BROUGHTON CASTLE
5034 CORFE CASTLE
5035 COITY CASTLE
5036 LYONSHALL CASTLE
5037 MONMOUTH CASTLE
5038 MORLAIS CASTLE
5039 RHUDDLAN CASTLE
5040 STOKESAY CASTLE
5041 TIVERTON CASTLE
5042 WINCHESTER CASTLE
5043 BARBURY CASTLE/
    EARL OF MOUNT EDGCUMBE
5044 BEVERSTON CASTLE/
    EARL OF DUNRAVEN
5045 BRIDGWATER CASTLE/
    EARL OF DUDLEY
5046 CLIFFORD CASTLE/
    EARL CAWDOR
5047 COMPTON CASTLE/
    EARL OF DARTMOUTH
5048 CRANBROOK CASTLE/
    EARL OF DEVON
5049 DENBIGH CASTLE/
    EARL OF PLYMOUTH
5050 DEVIZES CASTLE/
    EARL OF ST GERMANS
5051 DRYSLLWYN CASTLE/
    EARL BATHURST
5052 EASTNOR CASTLE/
    EARL OF RADNOR
5053 BISHOP'S CASTLE/
    EARL CAIRNS
5054 LAMPHEY CASTLE/
    EARL OF DUCIE
5055 LYDFORD CASTLE/
    EARL OF ELDON
5056 OGMORE CASTLE/
    EARL OF POWIS
5057 PENRICE CASTLE/
    EARL WALDEGRAVE
5058 NEWPORT CASTLE/
    EARL OF CLANCARTY
5059 POWIS CASTLE/
    EARL ST ALDWYN
5060 SARUM CASTLE/
    EARL OF BERKELEY
5061 SUDELEY CASTLE/
    EARL OF BIRKENHEAD
5062 TENBY CASTLE/
    EARL OF SHAFTESBURY
5063 THORNBURY CASTLE/
    EARL BALDWIN
5064 TRETOWER CASTLE/
    BISHOP'S CASTLE
5065 UPTON CASTLE/
    NEWPORT CASTLE
5066 WARDOUR CASTLE/
    SIR FELIX POLE
5067 ST FAGANS CASTLE
5068 BEVERSTON CASTLE
5069 ISAMBARD KINGDOM BRUNEL
5070 SIR DANIEL GOOCH
5071 CLIFFORD CASTLE/SPITFIRE
5072 COMPTON CASTLE/
    HURRICANE
5073 CRANBROOK CASTLE/
    BLENHEIM
5074 DENBIGH CASTLE/
    HAMPDEN

5075 DEVIZES CASTLE/
    WELLINGTON
5076 DRYSLLWYN CASTLE/
    GLADIATOR
5077 EASTNOR CASTLE/
    FAIREY BATTLE
5078 LAMPHEY CASTLE/
    BEAUFORT
5079 LYDFORD CASTLE/
    LYSANDER
5080 OGMORE CASTLE/DEFIANT
5081 PENRICE CASTLE/
    LOCKHEED HUDSON
5082 POWIS CASTLE/SWORDFISH
5083 BATH ABBEY
5084 READING ABBEY
5085 EVESHAM ABBEY
5086 VISCOUNT HORNE
5087 TINTERN ABBEY
5088 LLANTHONY ABBEY
5089 WESTMINSTER ABBEY
5090 NEATH ABBEY
5091 CLEEVE ABBEY
5092 TRESCO ABBEY
5093 UPTON CASTLE
5094 TRETOWER CASTLE
5095 BARBURY CASTLE
5096 BRIDGWATER CASTLE
5097 SARUM CASTLE
5098 CLIFFORD CASTLE
5099 COMPTON CASTLE
7000 VISCOUNT PORTAL
7001 DENBIGH CASTLE/
    SIR JAMES MILNE
7002 DEVIZES CASTLE
7003 ELMLEY CASTLE
7004 EASTNOR CASTLE
7005 LAMPHEY CASTLE/
    SIR EDWARD ELGAR
7006 LYDFORD CASTLE
7007 OGMORE CASTLE/
    GREAT WESTERN *
7008 SWANSEA CASTLE
7009 ATHELNEY CASTLE
7010 AVONDALE CASTLE
7011 BANBURY CASTLE
7012 BARRY CASTLE
7013 BRISTOL CASTLE
7014 CAERHAYS CASTLE
7015 CARN BREA CASTLE
7016 CHESTER CASTLE
7017 G.J. CHURCHWARD
7018 DRYSLLWYN CASTLE
7019 FOWEY CASTLE
7020 GLOUCESTER CASTLE
7021 HAVERFORDWEST CASTLE
7022 HEREFORD CASTLE
7023 PENRICE CASTLE
7024 POWIS CASTLE
7025 SUDELEY CASTLE
7026 TENBY CASTLE
7027 THORNBURY CASTLE
7028 CADBURY CASTLE
7029 CLUN CASTLE
7030 CRANBROOK CASTLE
7031 CROMWELL'S CASTLE
7032 DENBIGH CASTLE
7033 HARTLEBURY CASTLE
7034 INCE CASTLE
7035 OGMORE CASTLE
7036 TAUNTON CASTLE
7037 SWINDON *

These locomotives carried either a brass regimental crest or a transferred coat of arms on the splasher below the nameplate.

16

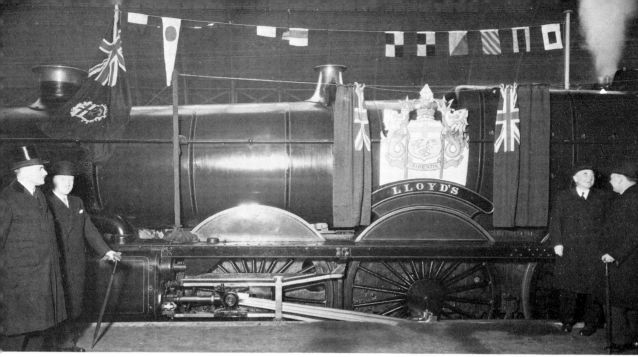

British Rail

THE NAMING CEREMONY OF "LLOYD'S"

As with shipping companies naming their vessels at ceremonious launchings, the railways also took advantage wherever possible of holding naming ceremonies for their locomotives. It was an auspicious occasion at Paddington Station on February 17th, 1936, when a 'Castle' class engine was officially named **LLOYD'S** and numbered 100 A1. The ceremony was performed by Viscount Horne, Chairman of the G.W.R. in the presence of officials from Lloyds.

Our photograph depicts the scene shortly after the unveiling of the nameplate, which was by means of two Red Ensigns. The plate was surmounted by a large replica of Lloyd's coat of arms, and above the locomotive were naval code flags spelling out "A1 AT LLOYDS". This locomotive was originally a 'Star' class engine No.4009 **SHOOTING STAR**, but was rebuilt as a 'Castle' in 1925, and retained its original name until renamed as above in 1936.

No.5034. Unlike the earlier classes, the short 'Castle' names were not spaced out. *J. Oatway*

No.7002. The only 'Castle' with a 'Z'. *B. Hilton*

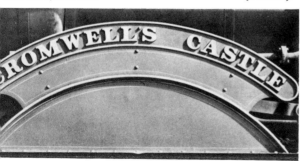

No.7031 with the smaller apostrophe. *Photomatic*

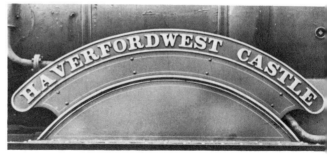

No.7021. One of the long plates requiring four supporting brackets. *Photomatic*

No.4000, one of the rebuilt 'Star' class. *G.O.P. Pearce*

NAME VARIATIONS
of the 'Castle' Class

Although called the 'Castle' class, it is surprising to find that 59 of the 171 engines were at some time or other named after anything but Castles! It was indeed a very mixed class which included Stars, Regiments, Earls, Personalities, Aircraft and Abbeys.

Actually, 40 engines lost their 'Castle' names to make way for some of the variations, but many of them reappeared on subsequent locomotives.

No.7007. One of two in the class to display a coat of arms below the nameplate. *D.H. Cape*

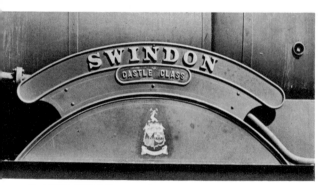

No.7037. Officially named by Princess Elizabeth on November 15th, 1950 at Swindon Works Erecting Shop in honour of the Borough's Jubilee. A commemorative plate was also fitted to the left-hand cabside. *Photomatic*

No.5071. One of the 'Castles' renamed during the war after well-known aircraft. *C.L. Caddy*

No.4037. Previously named QUEEN PHILIPPA, this locomotive was officially renamed *as above* on April 14th, 1937. *R.C. Riley*

No.5017. Originally ST DONATS CASTLE, it was officially renamed on April 24th, 1954 to commemorate the regiment's part in the Korean war. *R.O. Coffin*

No.4016. At first named KNIGHT OF THE GOLDEN FLEECE, it was officially renamed *as above* on February 18th, 1938. The small letters measured $1\frac{7}{8}$ in. high at face (see page 13).

A.R. Goult

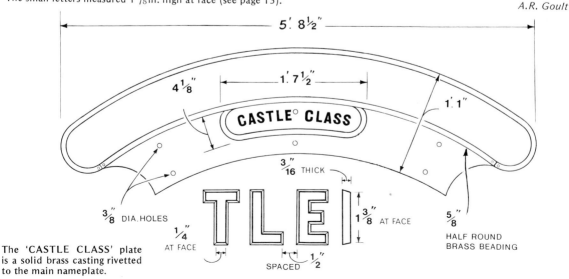

The 'CASTLE CLASS' plate is a solid brass casting rivetted to the main nameplate.

Note: The above is based on an official drawing and some variations may be found on the actual nameplates.

19

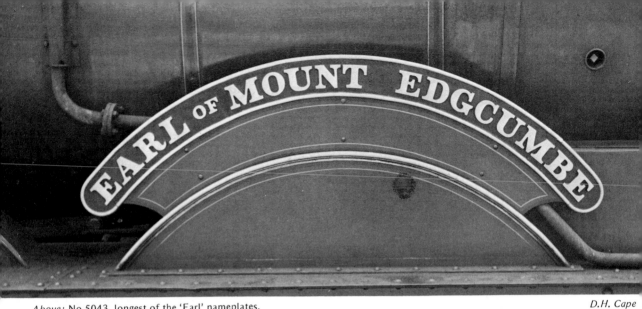

Above: No.5043, longest of the 'Earl' nameplates.

D.H. Cape

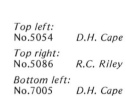

The 'Earl' plates were of a smaller radius; some having been transferred from the 4-4-0's of the '3200' class.

Top left:
No.5054   *D.H. Cape*

Top right:
No.5086   *R.C. Riley*

Bottom left:
No.7005   *D.H. Cape*

Bottom right:
No.5090   *A. Delicata*

Below: The naming ceremony of No.7017 held at Paddington Station on October 29th, 1948. The only nameplate in the class with full stops. They measure $^{7}/_{16}$ in. sq. at face.

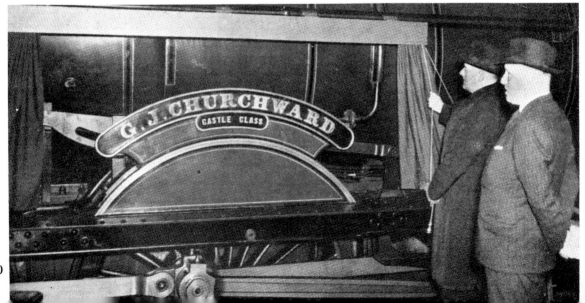

With the Great Western Railway's reputation for consistent design, it was rather a surprise in March, 1935, when two of their locomotives emerged semi-streamlined. One of them was a 'Castle' No.5005 MANORBIER CASTLE and the other a 'King'. However, the standard nameplates were refitted by August, 1946, and eventually, the other trimmings were removed. *British Rail Photos*

Another unsightly example which did not last long! When No.5069 was built in June, 1938, the G.W.R. decided to name it after their renowned pioneer engineer. Because of its length, they first fitted a unique large radius nameplate.

Somehow, it just didn't look right, and was replaced by a more pleasing nameplate of orthodox pattern in July, 1938.

Left: By courtesy of L. & G.R. Photos
Below: J. Oatway

No.6000 as originally built in 1927   *British Rail*

'KING' CLASS

6000 KING GEORGE V	6011 KING JAMES I	6022 KING EDWARD III
6001 KING EDWARD VII	6012 KING EDWARD VI	6023 KING EDWARD II
6002 KING WILLIAM IV	6013 KING HENRY VIII	6024 KING EDWARD I
6003 KING GEORGE IV	6014 KING HENRY VII	6025 KING HENRY III
6004 KING GEORGE III	6015 KING RICHARD III	6026 KING JOHN
6005 KING GEORGE II	6016 KING EDWARD V	6027 KING RICHARD I
6006 KING GEORGE I	6017 KING EDWARD IV	6028 KING HENRY II/
6007 KING WILLIAM III	6018 KING HENRY VI	KING GEORGE VI
6008 KING JAMES II	6019 KING HENRY V	6029 KING STEPHEN/
6009 KING CHARLES II	6020 KING HENRY IV	KING EDWARD VIII
6010 KING CHARLES I	6021 KING RICHARD II	

No.6002 in final form with double chimney and B.R. livery.   *Photomatic*

The 'King' class was introduced in 1927 and completed by 1930. The thirty locomotives were the largest of all Great Western 4-6-0's, and the most powerful passenger engines in the country at that time. Here we see a dramatic shot of the nameplate fitted to No.6024.   *G.O.P. Pearce*

THE ONE WITH THE BELL!

The most well-known 'King' of them all. Preserved No.6000 KING GEORGE V showing the famous bell presented during its visit to the Centenary Celebrations of the Baltimore and Ohio Railroad, U.S.A. in 1927.
Above: B. Stephenson   *Below: D.H. Cape*

No.6002   *S.R. Dewey*

No.6006   *J. Oatway*

No.6007   *S.R. Dewey*

No.6008   *J. Oatway*

No.6009   *British Rail*

No.6013   *J. Oatway*

No.6021   *J. Oatway*

25

In 1909, the names of Kings appeared as part of the 'Star' class, but these differed from those reviewed here because the letters were spaced out more and there were no Roman numerals after the names. Two examples are shown: No.4028 *above* and No.4029 *below*.

No.6026   J. Oatway

The numbers and names of the ten earlier 'Star' class Kings were as follows:

4021 KING EDWARD	4026 KING RICHARD
4022 KING WILLIAM	4027 KING HENRY
4023 KING GEORGE	4028 KING JOHN
4024 KING JAMES	4029 KING STEPHEN
4025 KING CHARLES	4030 KING HAROLD

'KINGS' RENAMED

When the 'King' class was introduced in 1927, the above 'Stars' were renamed as Monarchs to avoid confusion.

Even two of the 'King' class were renamed. In May, 1936, No.**6029** KING STEPHEN *shown on the right* received new nameplates for the uncrowned **KING EDWARD VIII**, and with his abdication a few months later, No.**6028** **KING HENRY II** became **KING GEORGE VI** in January 1937.

Both the new nameplates are shown below.

No.6029   British Rail

No.6028   J. Oatway

No.6029   R.C. Riley

STREAMLINING A 'KING'

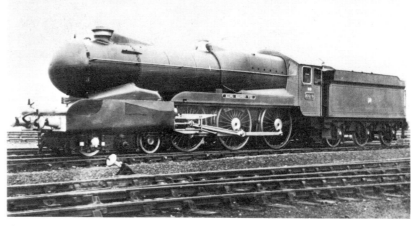

No.6014 as she appeared at Swindon in 1935.

British Rail Photos

In March, 1935, one of the class No.6014 KING HENRY VII was partially streamlined in similar fashion to No.5005 of the 'Castle' class. The experiment was not deemed a success, and over the years, piece by piece, most of the streamlining was removed. The straight nameplates, as with the 'Castle', were eventually replaced by the more conventional curved type by January 1943.

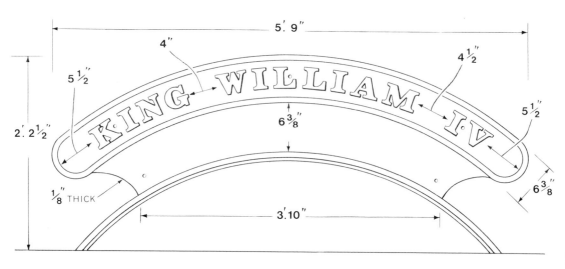

'HALL' CLASS

The prototype of the 'Hall' class, *as shown above,* appeared in 1924 as a rebuild of the 'Saint' class No.2925 SAINT MARTIN. It retained its name, and the number was not changed to 4900 until December, 1928. During that year, construction began of the 'Hall' class proper, and further engines were built, with modifications, right up to 1950.

Above: British Rail   Right: R.C. Riley

No.3951 ASHWICKE HALL   was one of eleven 'Halls' converted to oil burning in 1946/7, and renumbered in the 3900 series. They had all reverted to their original condition and their old numbers by April, 1950.   *British Rail*

Above: No.4920. It was the policy of the G.W.R. to display their names over the centre coupled wheels.
G.O.P. Pearce

Left: No.6990. This locomotive took part in the famous 1948 locomotive exchanges.
C.L. Caddy

No.7929   B. Hilton   No.4984   D.H. Cape

4900 SAINT MARTIN	4942 MAINDY HALL	4983 ALBERT HALL	5923 COLSTON HALL
4901 ADDERLEY HALL	4943 MARRINGTON HALL	4984 ALBRIGHTON HALL	5924 DINTON HALL
4902 ALDENHAM HALL	4944 MIDDLETON HALL	4985 ALLERSLEY HALL/	5925 EASTCOTE HALL
4903 ASTLEY HALL	4945 MILLIGAN HALL	ALLESLEY HALL	5926 GROTRIAN HALL
4904 BINNEGAR HALL	4946 MOSELEY HALL	4986 ASTON HALL	5927 GUILD HALL
4905 BARTON HALL	4947 NANHORAN HALL	4987 BROCKLEY HALL	5928 HADDON HALL
4906 BRADFIELD HALL	4948 NORTHWICK HALL	4988 BULWELL HALL	5929 HANHAM HALL
4907 BROUGHTON HALL	4949 PACKWOOD HALL	4989 CHERWELL HALL	5930 HANNINGTON HALL
4908 BROOME HALL	4950 PATSHULL HALL	4990 CLIFTON HALL	5931 HATHERLEY HALL
4909 BLAKESLEY HALL	4951 PENDEFORD HALL	4991 COBHAM HALL	5932 HAYDON HALL
4910 BLAISDON HALL	4952 PEPLOW HALL	4992 CROSBY HALL	5933 KINGSWAY HALL
4911 BOWDEN HALL	4953 PITCHFORD HALL	4993 DALTON HALL	5934 KNELLER HALL
4912 BERRINGTON HALL	4954 PLAISH HALL	4994 DOWNTON HALL	5935 NORTON HALL
4913 BAGLAN HALL	4955 PLASPOWER HALL	4995 EASTON HALL	5936 OAKLEY HALL
4914 CRANMORE HALL	4956 PLOWDEN HALL	4996 EDEN HALL	5937 STANFORD HALL
4915 CONDOVER HALL	4957 POSTLIP HALL	4997 ELTON HALL	5938 STANLEY HALL
4916 CRUMLIN HALL	4958 PRIORY HALL	4998 EYTON HALL	5939 TANGLEY HALL
4917 CROSSWOOD HALL	4959 PURLEY HALL	4999 GOPSAL HALL	5940 WHITBOURNE HALL
4918 DARTINGTON HALL	4960 PYLE HALL	5900 HINDERTON HALL	5941 CAMPION HALL
4919 DONNINGTON HALL	4961 PYRLAND HALL	5901 HAZEL HALL	5942 DOLDOWLOD HALL
4920 DUMBLETON HALL	4962 RAGLEY HALL	5902 HOWICK HALL	5943 ELMDON HALL
4921 EATON HALL	4963 RIGNALL HALL	5903 KEELE HALL	5944 ICKENHAM HALL
4922 ENVILLE HALL	4964 RODWELL HALL	5904 KELHAM HALL	5945 LECKHAMPTON HALL
4923 EVENLEY HALL	4965 ROOD ASHTON HALL	5905 KNOWSLEY HALL	5946 MARWELL HALL
4924 EYDON HALL	4966 SHAKENHURST HALL	5906 LAWTON HALL	5947 SAINT BENETS HALL/
4925 EYNSHAM HALL	4967 SHIRENEWTON HALL	5907 MARBLE HALL	SAINT BENET'S HALL
4926 FAIRLEIGH HALL	4968 SHOTTON HALL	5908 MORETON HALL	5948 SIDDINGTON HALL
4927 FARNBOROUGH HALL	4969 SHRUGBOROUGH HALL	5909 NEWTON HALL	5949 TREMATON HALL
4928 GATACRE HALL	4970 SKETTY HALL	5910 PARK HALL	5950 WARDLEY HALL
4929 GOYTREY HALL	4971 STANWAY HALL	5911 PRESTON HALL	5951 CLYFFE HALL
4930 HAGLEY HALL	4972 ST BRIDES HALL/	5912 QUEENS HALL/	5952 COGAN HALL
4931 HANBURY HALL	SAINT BRIDES HALL	QUEEN'S HALL	5953 DUNLEY HALL
4932 HATHERTON HALL	4973 SWEENEY HALL	5913 RUSHTON HALL	5954 FAENDRE HALL
4933 HIMLEY HALL	4974 TALGARTH HALL	5914 RIPON HALL	5955 GARTH HALL
4934 HINDLIP HALL	4975 UMBERSLADE HALL	5915 TRENTHAM HALL	5956 HORSLEY HALL
4935 KETLEY HALL	4976 WARFIELD HALL	5916 TRINITY HALL	5957 HUTTON HALL
4936 KINLET HALL	4977 WATCOMBE HALL	5917 WESTMINSTER HALL	5958 KNOLTON HALL
4937 LANELAY HALL	4978 WESTWOOD HALL	5918 WALTON HALL	5959 MAWLEY HALL
4938 LIDDINGTON HALL	4979 WOOTTON HALL	5919 WORSLEY HALL	5960 SAINT EDMUND HALL
4939 LITTLETON HALL	4980 WROTTESLEY HALL	5920 WYCLIFFE HALL	5961 TOYNBEE HALL
4940 LUDFORD HALL	4981 ABBERLEY HALL	5921 BINGLEY HALL	5962 WANTAGE HALL
4941 LLANGEDWYN HALL	4982 ACTON HALL	5922 CAXTON HALL	5963 WIMPOLE HALL

Below: No.7900 showing the smaller apostrophe.   *M.J. Robertson*

No.6972   B. Hilton   No.6991   D.H. Cape

5964 WOLSELEY HALL	6906 CHICHELEY HALL	6948 HOLBROOKE HALL	6990 WITHERSLACK HALL
5965 WOOLLAS HALL	6907 DAVENHAM HALL	6949 HABERFIELD HALL	6991 ACTON BURNELL HALL
5966 ASHFORD HALL	6908 DOWNHAM HALL	6950 KINGSTHORPE HALL	6992 ARBORFIELD HALL
5967 BICKMARSH HALL	6909 FREWIN HALL	6951 IMPNEY HALL	6993 ARTHOG HALL
5968 CORY HALL	6910 GOSSINGTON HALL	6952 KIMBERLEY HALL	6994 BAGGRAVE HALL
5969 HONINGTON HALL	6911 HOLKER HALL	6953 LEIGHTON HALL	6995 BENTHALL HALL
5970 HENGRAVE HALL	6912 HELMSTER HALL	6954 LOTHERTON HALL	6996 BLACKWELL HALL
5971 MEREVALE HALL	6913 LEVENS HALL	6955 LYDCOTT HALL	6997 BRYN-IVOR HALL
5972 OLTON HALL	6914 LANGTON HALL	6956 MOTTRAM HALL	6998 BURTON AGNES HALL
5973 ROLLESTON HALL	6915 MURSLEY HALL	6957 NORCLIFFE HALL	6999 CAPEL DEWI HALL
5974 WALLSWORTH HALL	6916 MISTERTON HALL	6958 OXBURGH HALL	7900 SAINT PETER'S HALL
5975 WINSLOW HALL	6917 OLDLANDS HALL	6959 PEATLING HALL	7901 DODINGTON HALL
5976 ASHWICKE HALL	6918 SANDON HALL	6960 RAVENINGHAM HALL	7902 EATON MASCOT HALL
5977 BECKFORD HALL	6919 TYLNEY HALL	6961 STEDHAM HALL	7903 FOREMARKE HALL
5978 BODINNICK HALL	6920 BARNINGHAM HALL	6962 SOUGHTON HALL	7904 FOUNTAINS HALL
5979 CRUCKTON HALL	6921 BORWICK HALL	6963 THROWLEY HALL	7905 FOWEY HALL
5980 DINGLEY HALL	6922 BURTON HALL	6964 THORNBRIDGE HALL	7906 FRON HALL
5981 FRENSHAM HALL	6923 CROXTETH HALL	6965 THIRLESTAINE HALL	7907 HART HALL
5982 HARRINGTON HALL	6924 GRANTLEY HALL	6966 WITCHINGHAM HALL	7908 HENSHALL HALL
5983 HENLEY HALL	6925 HACKNESS HALL	6967 WILLESLEY HALL	7909 HEVENINGHAM HALL
5984 LINDEN HALL	6926 HOLKHAM HALL	6968 WOODCOCK HALL	7910 HOWN HALL
5985 MOSTYN HALL	6927 LILFORD HALL	6969 WRAYSBURY HALL	7911 LADY MARGARET HALL
5986 ARBURY HALL	6928 UNDERLEY HALL	6970 WHADDON HALL	7912 LITTLE LINFORD HALL
5987 BROCKET HALL	6929 WHORLTON HALL	6971 ATHELHAMPTON HALL	7913 LITTLE WYRLEY HALL
5988 BOSTOCK HALL	6930 ALDERSEY HALL	6972 BENINGBROUGH HALL	7914 LLEWENI HALL
5989 CRANSLEY HALL	6931 ALDBOROUGH HALL	6973 BRICKLEHAMPTON HALL	7915 MERE HALL
5990 DORFORD HALL	6932 BURWARTON HALL	6974 BRYNGWYN HALL	7916 MOBBERLEY HALL
5991 GRESHAM HALL	6933 BIRTLES HALL	6975 CAPESTHORNE HALL	7917 NORTH ASTON HALL
5992 HORTON HALL	6934 BEACHAMWELL HALL	6976 GRAYTHWAITE HALL	7918 RHOSE WOOD HALL
5993 KIRBY HALL	6935 BROWSHOLME HALL	6977 GRUNDISBURGH HALL	7919 RUNTER HALL
5994 ROYDON HALL	6936 BRECCLES HALL	6978 HAROLDSTONE HALL	7920 CONEY HALL
5995 WICK HALL	6937 CONYNGHAM HALL	6979 HELPERLY HALL	7921 EDSTONE HALL
5996 MYTTON HALL	6938 CORNDEAN HALL	6980 LLANRUMNEY HALL	7922 SALFORD HALL
5997 SPARKFORD HALL	6939 CALVELEY HALL	6981 MARBURY HALL	7923 SPEKE HALL
5998 TREVOR HALL	6940 DIDLINGTON HALL	6982 MELMERBY HALL	7924 THORNYCROFT HALL
5999 WOLLATON HALL	6941 FILLONGLEY HALL	6983 OTTERINGTON HALL	7925 WESTOL HALL
6900 ABNEY HALL	6942 ESHTON HALL	6984 OWSDEN HALL	7926 WILLEY HALL
6901 ARLEY HALL	6943 FARNLEY HALL	6985 PARWICK HALL	7927 WILLINGTON HALL
6902 BUTLERS HALL	6944 FLEDBOROUGH HALL	6986 RYDAL HALL	7928 WOLF HALL
6903 BELMONT HALL	6945 GLASFRYN HALL	6987 SHERVINGTON HALL	7929 WYKE HALL
6904 CHARFIELD HALL	6946 HEATHERDEN HALL	6988 SWITHLAND HALL	
6905 CLAUGHTON HALL	6947 HELMINGHAM HALL	6989 WIGHTWICK HALL	

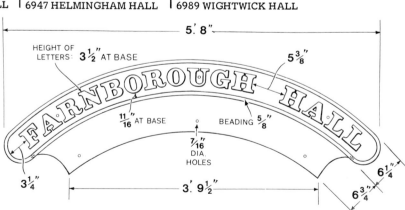

Note: Owing to economic conditions prevailing at the time, many of the latter engines had plates with only half-round beading at the top. On these, the overall measurement from the top line of beading to the bottom was only 6in. and not 6¼in. as above.

31

First of the class No.6800 outside Swindon Works in August 1936.

British Rail

'GRANGE' CLASS

Built between 1936 and 1939, the 4-6-0 'Grange' class were designed to replace the older 2-6-0's. In fact, the wheels and motion from the '4300' class locomotives were used in their construction. It was intended to build many more, but the war caused the programme to be postponed.

6800 ARLINGTON GRANGE	6820 KINGSTONE GRANGE	6840 HAZELEY GRANGE	6860 ABERPORTH GRANGE
6801 AYLBURTON GRANGE	6821 LEATON GRANGE	6841 MARLAS GRANGE	6861 CRYNANT GRANGE
6802 BAMPTON GRANGE	6822 MANTON GRANGE	6842 NUNHOLD GRANGE	6862 DERWENT GRANGE
6803 BUCKLEBURY GRANGE	6823 OAKLEY GRANGE	6843 POULTON GRANGE	6863 DOLHYWEL GRANGE
6804 BROCKINGTON GRANGE	6824 ASHLEY GRANGE	6844 PENHYDD GRANGE	6864 DYMOCK GRANGE
6805 BROUGHTON GRANGE	6825 LLANVAIR GRANGE	6845 PAVILAND GRANGE	6865 HOPTON GRANGE
6806 BLACKWELL GRANGE	6826 NANNERTH GRANGE	6846 RUCKLEY GRANGE	6866 MORFA GRANGE
6807 BIRCHWOOD GRANGE	6827 LLANFRECHFA GRANGE	6847 TIDMARSH GRANGE	6867 PETERSTON GRANGE
6808 BEENHAM GRANGE	6828 TRELLECH GRANGE	6848 TODDINGTON GRANGE	6868 PENRHOS GRANGE
6809 BURGHCLERE GRANGE	6829 BURMINGTON GRANGE	6849 WALTON GRANGE	6869 RESOLVEN GRANGE
6810 BLAKEMERE GRANGE	6830 BUCKENHILL GRANGE	6850 CLEEVE GRANGE	6870 BODICOTE GRANGE
6811 CRANBOURNE GRANGE	6831 BEARLEY GRANGE	6851 HURST GRANGE	6871 BOURTON GRANGE
6812 CHESFORD GRANGE	6832 BROCKTON GRANGE	6852 HEADBOURNE GRANGE	6872 CRAWLEY GRANGE
6813 EASTBURY GRANGE	6833 CALCOT GRANGE	6853 MOREHAMPTON GRANGE	6873 CARADOC GRANGE
6814 ENBORNE GRANGE	6834 DUMMER GRANGE	6854 ROUNDHILL GRANGE	6874 HAUGHTON GRANGE
6815 FRILFORD GRANGE	6835 EASTHAM GRANGE	6855 SAIGHTON GRANGE	6875 HINDFORD GRANGE
6816 FRANKTON GRANGE	6836 ESTEVARNEY GRANGE	6856 STOWE GRANGE	6876 KINGSLAND GRANGE
6817 GWENDDWR GRANGE	6837 FORTHAMPTON GRANGE	6857 TUDOR GRANGE	6877 LLANFAIR GRANGE
6818 HARDWICK GRANGE	6838 GOODMOOR GRANGE	6858 WOOLSTON GRANGE	6878 LONGFORD GRANGE
6819 HIGHNAM GRANGE	6839 HEWELL GRANGE	6859 YIEWSLEY GRANGE	6879 OVERTON GRANGE

Below: No.6829

D.H. Cape

No.6847   *D.H. Cape*

No.6851   *R.C. Riley*

No.6860   *J. Alsop*

No.6825   *B. Hilton*

No.6838   *D.H. Cape*

33

This view of 'Manor' No.7805 provides an interesting comparison with the 'Grange' on page 32.
British Rail

'MANOR' CLASS

The first 'Manors' appeared in 1938 as a lighter version of the 'Granges', thus providing greater route availability. As with the previous class, the war intervened, and the last ten 'Manors' were not built until 1950 after Nationalisation. In the later years, certain improvements were carried out to the blast pipe which resulted in a chimney without the deflector rim *as shown on the right.*

7800 TORQUAY MANOR	7810 DRAYCOTT MANOR	7820 DINMORE MANOR
7801 ANTHONY MANOR	7811 DUNLEY MANOR	7821 DITCHEAT MANOR
7802 BRADLEY MANOR	7812 ERLESTOKE MANOR	7822 FOXCOTE MANOR
7803 BARCOTE MANOR	7813 FRESHFORD MANOR	7823 HOOK NORTON MANOR
7804 BAYDON MANOR	7814 FRINGFORD MANOR	7824 IFORD MANOR
7805 BROOME MANOR	7815 FRITWELL MANOR	7825 LECHLADE MANOR
7806 COCKINGTON MANOR	7816 FRILSHAM MANOR	7826 LONGWORTH MANOR
7807 COMPTON MANOR	7817 GARSINGTON MANOR	7827 LYDHAM MANOR
7808 COOKHAM MANOR	7818 GRANVILLE MANOR	7828 ODNEY MANOR
7809 CHILDREY MANOR	7819 HINTON MANOR	7829 RAMSBURY MANOR

Below: First of the class, No.7800.   *D.H. Cape*

No.7801   *L. Hanson*

No.7803   *C.L. Caddy*

No.7818   *D.H. Cape*

No.7810   *D.H. Cape*

Below: Longest name in the class, No.7823   *D.H. Cape*

No.1029 as originally built with traditional single chimney.   *British Ra*

'COUNTY' CLASS

The thirty 'Counties' were constructed between 1945 and 1947, and were the most powerful two-cylinder 4-6-0's to run on the G.W.R. The earlier 4-4-0 'County' class of 1904 had forty engines all with curved nameplates.

1000 COUNTY OF MIDDLESEX
1001 COUNTY OF BUCKS
1002 COUNTY OF BERKS
1003 COUNTY OF WILTS
1004 COUNTY OF SOMERSET
1005 COUNTY OF DEVON
1006 COUNTY OF CORNWALL
1007 COUNTY OF BRECKNOCK
1008 COUNTY OF CARDIGAN
1009 COUNTY OF CARMARTHEN
1010 COUNTY OF CARNARVON/
     COUNTY OF CAERNARVON
1011 COUNTY OF CHESTER
1012 COUNTY OF DENBIGH
1013 COUNTY OF DORSET
1014 COUNTY OF GLAMORGAN
1015 COUNTY OF GLOUCESTER
1016 COUNTY OF HANTS
1017 COUNTY OF HEREFORD
1018 COUNTY OF LEICESTER
1019 COUNTY OF MERIONETH
1020 COUNTY OF MONMOUTH
1021 COUNTY OF MONTGOMERY
1022 COUNTY OF NORTHAMPTON
1023 COUNTY OF OXFORD
1024 COUNTY OF PEMBROKE
1025 COUNTY OF RADNOR
1026 COUNTY OF SALOP
1027 COUNTY OF STAFFORD
1028 COUNTY OF WARWICK
1029 COUNTY OF WORCESTER

In 1956, work started on fitting the class with squat double chimneys, which whilst improving the efficiency did nothing for their appearance!   *British Rail*

Above: The left-hand side of No.1006 showing the nameplate fitted to the splasher. *G.O.P. Pearce*

Below: Because of the reversing gear on the right-hand side, the name was displayed on an extended backplate as shown here on No.1017. *L.M. Hobdey*

No.1013 Right-hand side.   *C.L. Caddy*

No.1013 Left-hand side.   *F.B.*

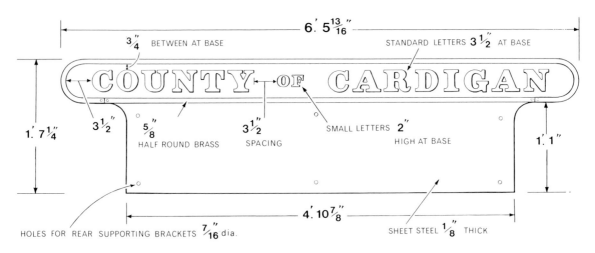

6.' 5$\frac{13}{16}$"

$\frac{3}{4}$" BETWEEN AT BASE

STANDARD LETTERS 3$\frac{1}{2}$" AT BASE

1.' 7$\frac{1}{4}$"

3$\frac{1}{2}$"

$\frac{5}{8}$"
HALF ROUND BRASS

3$\frac{1}{2}$"
SPACING

SMALL LETTERS 2"
HIGH AT BASE

1.' 1"

HOLES FOR REAR SUPPORTING BRACKETS $\frac{7}{16}$" dia.

4.' 10$\frac{7}{8}$"

SHEET STEEL $\frac{1}{8}$" THICK

The above dimensions were taken from the actual nameplate.
Officially, the length allocated for the plates were as follows:—
Counties with 5 or 6 letters   ....   6'0" long,
Counties with 7 or 8 letters   ....   6'6" long,
Counties with 9, 10 or 11 letters   ....   7'3" long.
However, there are variations to be found of up to ½in. depending on whether the plates had full or half-round beading.

Below: No.1019. One of the 7'3" full-beaded nameplates.   *D.H. Cape*

THE YEARS BEFORE 1923

Numerous companies were amalgamated to form the Southern Railway in 1923. Reviewed here, are some of the various styles these railways adopted to name their locomotives.

1847 brought a famous name to the London, Brighton & South Coast Railway in the shape of a 2-2-2 type engine built for them by E.B. Wilson & Co. of the Railway Foundry Leeds. No.60 **JENNY LIND.** later became No.70.

In the mid-1850's, the London & South Western Railway fitted unique curved nameplates to the cabsides of many of their locomotives. Two examples are shown of the same 2-4-0 type engine.

The original plates were changed when the engine was later re-boilered. In most cases, both the number and original building dates were included on the plates.

British Rail Photo

From the 1860's, the London, Chatham & Dover Railway started to fit rectangular plates to the forward part of the boiler sides. This 0-4-2 type engine, ERIN was built in 1873.

L. & G.R.P.

Also in the mid-1860's, a few L.C. & D.R. classes had the plates fitted to the centre of the boiler sides. Above one of six 0-6-0 engines turned out in 1866. *O.J. Morris*

It was the practice of the L.B. & S.C.R. to use hand-applied letters for their named locomotives. The first letter of each name was larger than the rest.

Both these engines, **BOXHILL** of 1880 and **GLADSTONE** of 1882 show the style used for the tank sides or wheel splashers.

When the Southern Railway came into being in 1923, they inherited many small dock engines, most of which carried names on the tank sides. Two engines dating back to 1878, VULCAN and her sister engine BRETWALDA, were originally taken over by the L. & S.W.R. when the Southampton Docks were absorbed in December, 1891. The two engines were sold by the S.R. in 1924 and 1926 respectively.

Photos right and below: H.C. Casserley

Two popular tank engines of the docks were IRONSIDE and its sister engine CLAUSENTUM, the latter being the Roman name for Southampton. They first saw service in 1890 and survived longer than most! IRONSIDE, in fact, was not withdrawn until 1954.

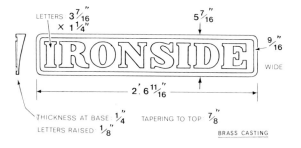

In 1891, the L. & S.W.R. introduced a new class of 0-4-0 tank engines. Most of them ran in the Southampton Docks; their names being painted or transferred onto the tank sides.

Lens of Sutton

The Lynton & Barnstaple Railway had narrow gauge tank engines named after local rivers. Four were built in 1897/9 and a fifth, Lᴇᴡ was added by the S.R. in 1925.

Odd man out on the Lynton & Barnstaple was this 2-4-2 tank built in 1899 by Baldwins of the U.S.A. Originally, it had LYN painted on the cabside, but this was later replaced by a brass plate. The other engines were 2-6-2T's which had their nameplates fitted to the tank sides. *Lens of Sutton*

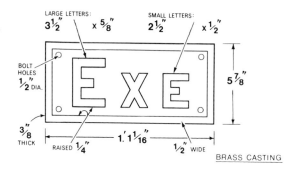

The Plymouth, Devonport & South Western Junction Railway, has three named tank engines which were absorbed by the S.R. *Above:* 0-6-0T **A.S. HARRIS**, built in 1907 by Hawthorn, Leslie & Co. of Newcastle-on-Tyne. *British Rail*

NAMEPLATES ON THE ISLE OF WIGHT

The Cowes and Newport Railway was the first of three lines on the Island, and PIONEER above, was its first engine. This, and its sister engine, PRECURSOR, were built by Slaughter, Gruning & Co. of Bristol in 1861, and ran in 1862 when the line was opened. Both these 2-2-2 type locomotives survived until 1904.   *British Rail*

This close-up of PIONEER's sister engine, shows the large safety valve cover added later to the boiler. Both locomotives were also given a cab and shorter chimney.
O.J. Morris

Below are listed the named locomotives in service at the time of the 1923 amalgamation into the Southern Railway. Some of these names were subsequently transferred to other engines, which had hitherto been unnamed.

COWES	Isle of Wight Central Rly. Remained No.4 ...*scrapped 1925*
OSBORNE	Isle of Wight Central Rly. Remained No.5 ...*scrapped 1926*
SANDOWN	Isle of Wight Rly. Remained unnumbered ...*scrapped 1923*
RYDE	Isle of Wight Rly. Became first S.R.No. w13 *withdrawn 1932*
SHANKLIN	Isle of Wight Rly. Became first S.R.No. w14...*scrapped 1927*
VENTNOR	Isle of Wight Rly. Became first S.R.No. w15...*scrapped 1925*
WROXALL	Isle of Wight Rly. Became first S.R.No. w16...*scrapped 1933*
BRADING	Isle of Wight Rly. Became first S.R.No. w17...*scrapped 1926*
BONCHURCH.	Isle of Wight Rly. Became first S.R.No. w18...*scrapped 1928*

The Isle of Wight Railway, opened in 1864, only named their tank engines. Above: BRADING which later became S.R. No. w17.   *Real Photo*

The close-up pictures, above and on the right, are in proportion. WROXALL first had small nameplates with square-cut ends, and when the S.R. took over they added rather large 'SOUTHERN' letters and numerals to the tank sides.

Later, the plates were replaced by larger standard ones. The 'SOUTHERN' lettering was made smaller and the numerals were transferred to the bunker sides.
Photos: Lens of Sutton

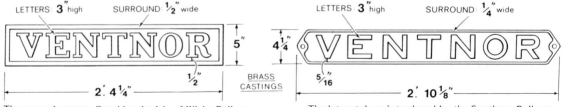

LETTERS: 3" high   SURROUND: ½" wide   5"   BRASS CASTINGS   4¼"   LETTERS: 3" high   SURROUND: ¼" wide

VENTNOR   ½"   2' 4¼"   5/16"   VENTNOR   2' 10⅛"

The normal pattern fitted by the Isle of Wight Railway.   The later style as introduced by the Southern Railway.

THE FINAL CLASSES OF THE I.O.W...

No. w1 MEDINA

'E1' CLASS

w1 MEDINA
w2 YARMOUTH
w3 RYDE
w4 WROXALL

This class was made up of former L.B.S.C.R. 0-6-0 tank engines, built between 1878 and 1881. Transferred to the I.O.W. 1932/33. *Note:* As some of the older types were scrapped or returned to the mainland, it was the practice of the Southern Railway to transfer the nameplates to the next, newly arrived locomotives.

No. w12 VENTNOR

Lens of Sutton

'A1X' CLASS

w8 FRESHWATER
w9 FISHBOURNE*
w10 COWES
w11 NEWPORT
w12 VENTNOR
w13 CARISBROOKE*
w14 BEMBRIDGE*

All built between 1874 and 1880, these 0-6-0 tank engines, like the previous class, first saw service with the L.B.S.C.R. but were purchased by two of the Island's Railways between 1900 and 1913. Those marked* did not arrive until 1927/30 having been transferred by the Southern Railway. All seven were returned to the mainland from 1936 to 1949.

No. w27 MERSTONE

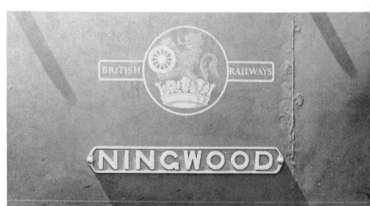

C.L. Caddy

'O2' CLASS

w14 FISHBOURNE	w22 BRADING	w30 SHORWELL
w15 COWES	w23 TOTLAND	w31 CHALE
w16 VENTNOR	w24 CALBOURNE	w32 BONCHURCH
w17 SEAVIEW	w25 GODSHILL	w33 BEMBRIDGE
w18 NINGWOOD	w26 WHITWELL	w34 NEWPORT
w19 OSBORNE	w27 MERSTONE	w35 FRESHWATER
w20 SHANKLIN	w28 ASHEY	w36 CARISBROOKE
w21 SANDOWN	w29 ALVERSTONE	

The tank locomotives of this final class, with an 0-4-4 wheel arrangement, were built by the L.S.W.R. between 1889 and 1892. They came to the Island usually in pairs over the years starting in 1923 to replace the other classes. The last two No's. w35 and w36 were in fact, transferred from the mainland by British Railways in 1949. Eleven new names were introduced with this class, the rest having previously been on older locomotives which the 'O2's' replaced.

Locomotive photos by Lens of Sutton

43

'H 1' CLASS

This 4-4-2 type first appeared in 1905 with the L.B. & S.C.R. The five locomotives were highly regarded in their day. However, until Southern days, they ran without names, except for No.39, which was named **LA FRANCE** in 1913 when it hauled a train carrying the President of France.

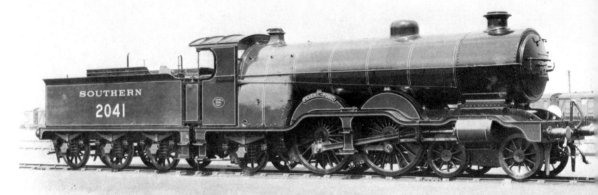

Soon after the Southern took over the L.B. & S.C.R., they decided to give names to both the 'H 1' and 'H 2' classes. Neat nameplates were fitted to the rear splashers.

Lens of Sutton

'H 2' CLASS

In 1911, a second batch of 4-4-2 engines was introduced, but these had a straighter frame. Like the previous class they were not given nameplates until Southern days. During their lifetime, both classes had a variety of chimneys fitted, the S.R. version being larger.

Left: British Rail   Below: Lens of Sutton

S.R. No.2040. One of the 'H 1' class that did not see B.R. service.   *A.G. Williamson by courtesy of R.C. Riley*

'H 1' CLASS
32037 SELSEY BILL
32038 PORTLAND BILL
32039 HARTLAND POINT
 2040 ST. CATHERINE'S POINT
 2041 PEVERIL POINT

'H 2' CLASS
32421 SOUTH FORELAND
32422 NORTH FORELAND
 2423 THE NEEDLES*
32424 BEACHY HEAD
32425 TREVOSE HEAD
32426 ST. ALBAN'S HEAD

Although this locomotive survived until B.R. days it was not renumbered.

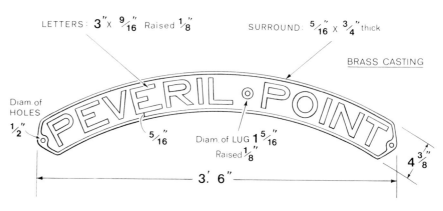

LETTERS: $3''$ x $\frac{9}{16}''$ Raised $\frac{1}{8}''$

SURROUND: $\frac{5}{16}$ x $\frac{3}{4}''$ thick

BRASS CASTING

Diam. of HOLES $\frac{1}{2}''$

$\frac{5}{16}''$

Diam. of LUG $1\frac{5}{16}''$ Raised $\frac{1}{8}''$

$4\frac{3}{8}''$

$3'\ 6''$

The specifications were identical for nameplates of both classes.

S.R. No.2423   *F.B.*

B.R. No.32424   *B. Hilton*

Between 1914 and 1922, the L.B. & S.C.R. built seven large 4-6-4 Baltic type tank engines. However, only three were named, and these were displayed by means of large letters on the tank sides. REMEMBRANCE, *shown on the left*, also had a brass plaque fitted below the name. Eventually, the names of the last two were replaced by straight cast nameplates. Between 1934 and 1936, owing to the electrification of the Brighton line, they were each rebuilt as 4-6-0 type tender locomotives for service on other routes. Except for No.2333 all received names of early locomotive designers.

Photos by Lens of Sutton

'REMEMBRANCE' CLASS

ORIGINAL TANK ENGINES
B327 (later 2327) CHARLES C. MACRAE.
B328 (later 2328)   —
B329 (later 2329) STEPHENSON.
B330 (later 2330)   —
B331 (later 2331)   —
B332 (later 2332)   —
B333 (later 2333) REMEMBRANCE

AS TENDER LOCOMOTIVES
2327 (later 32327) TREVITHICK
2328 (later 32328) HACKWORTH
2329 (later 32329) STEPHENSON
2330 (later 32330) CUDWORTH
2331 (later 32331) BEATTIE
2332 (later 32332) STROUDLEY
2333 (later 32333) REMEMBRANCE

The prefix B denotes Brighton

Above: REMEMBRANCE as she appeared with brass nameplates.

Above: The same locomotive as rebuilt with tender, and classified 'N15X'.

No.32333. The brass plaque under the nameplate was transferred from the original tank engine. It measured $17^3/_8$in. wide by $8^3/_8$in. deep. The letters were $^5/_8$in. high.

M.J. Robertson

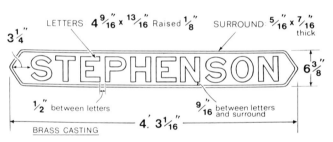

LETTERS $4^9/_{16}$″ × $^{13}/_{16}$″ Raised $^1/_8$″ SURROUND $^5/_{16}$″ × $^7/_{16}$″ thick

$3^1/_4$″

$6^3/_8$″

$^1/_2$″ between letters

$^9/_{16}$″ between letters and surround

4′ $3^1/_{16}$″

BRASS CASTING

The original nameplate as fitted to the S.R. tank engine No.2329.

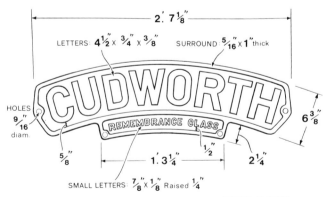

2′ $7^1/_8$″

LETTERS $4^1/_2$″ × $^3/_4$″ × $^3/_8$″ SURROUND $^5/_{16}$″ × 1″ thick

HOLES $^9/_{16}$″ diam.

$6^3/_8$″

$^5/_8$″

1′ $3^1/_4$″

$^1/_2$″

$2^1/_4$″

SMALL LETTERS: $^7/_8$″ × $^1/_8$″ Raised $^1/_4$″

BRASS CASTING

No.32329 *Photomatic*

No.32327 *G.O.P. Pearce*

No.32331 *R.C. Riley*

'RIVER' CLASS

The first locomotive of this 2-6-4T class was built by the S.E. & C.R. in 1917, and ran unnamed until the Southern grouping. Between 1925 and 1926, nineteen further locomotives were constructed. Each of these 'K' class engines was given the name of a river. An additional locomotive built with three cylinders was Classified 'K1'.

The first of class to be built. Unnamed in S.E. & C.R. days.

Photo: Ken Nunn Collection by courtesy of L.C.G.B.

Above: No. A807 RIVER AXE

Photos above and below: Ian Allan Library

Right: No. A890 RIVER FROME, the only one built as a 3-cylinder engine. It had a different front end and side appearance to the others, including a wider chimney.

A 790 RIVER AVON
A 791 RIVER ADUR
A 792 RIVER ARUN
A 793 RIVER OUSE
A 794 RIVER ROTHER
A 795 RIVER MEDWAY
A 796 RIVER STOUR
A 797 RIVER MOLE
A 798 RIVER WEY
A 799 RIVER TEST
A 800 RIVER CRAY
A 801 RIVER DARENTH
A 802 RIVER CUCKMERE
A 803 RIVER ITCHEN
A 804 RIVER TAMAR
A 805 RIVER CAMEL
A 806 RIVER TORRIDGE
A 807 RIVER AXE
A 808 RIVER CHAR
A 809 RIVER DART
A 890 RIVER FROME

The prefix A *denotes Ashford*

No. A793

Nameplate photos above and below: Ian Allan Library

No. A791   (¾-view)

The nameplates were of a similar pattern to those fitted to the tank engines of the 'Remembrance' class.

Right: Owing to a severe accident at Sevenoaks in 1927, in which one of the class, No. A800 RIVER CRAY was involved, it was decided to rebuild the whole class as 2-6-0 tender locomotives. The final result is shown on the right. It is rather ironic that this engine, B.R. No. 31790, finished up as it started — *nameless!* This was the first of the class to be built as seen at the top of the previous page.

Photo: C.P. Boocock

Above: No.740 (then unnamed) as it first appeared in L.S.W.R. livery, March, 1919. Built by Urie, this and nineteen others eventually became part of the 'King Arthur' class. The stove-pipe chimney lasted until Southern days.   *Lens of Sutton*

Left: S.R. No.4 (later B.R. No.304 SIR TRISTRAM of ten constructed Eastleigh in 1925. They were given th tenders from th scrapped Drummon 4-6-0's. These ha no outside axl boxes. From 195 to 1958 however they were replace with the heavie Urie-type tenders
Maurice Earley Collection

'KING ARTHUR' CLASS

Seventy-four locomotives made up this popular class. Comprising four types, each one having its own characteristics, they formed the main-stay of the Southern Railway well into the 1930's.

Above: S.R. No.784 (later B.R. No. 30784) SIR NEROVENS was one of the large group built by the North British Locomotive Company at their Hyde Park Works, Glasgow in 1925. Each of the thirty engines had a restyled cab roof.

Left: The final fourteen locomotives were built at Eastleigh in 1926/27. They all had six-wheeled, straight-sided tenders. The smoke deflectors were eventually fitted to the whole class.

Photos by Lens of Sutton

No.30453. It was the practice of the Southern Railway to include the 'Class' name in a small appendage below the plate, except for the one after which the class was named. *J. Oatway*

'EASTLEIGH' ARTHURS

30448 SIR TRISTRAM
30449 SIR TORRE
30450 SIR KAY
30451 SIR LAMORAK
30452 SIR MELIAGRANCE
30453 KING ARTHUR
30454 QUEEN GUINEVERE
30455 SIR LAUNCELOT
30456 SIR GALAHAD
30457 SIR BEDIVERE

'URIE' ARTHURS

30736 EXCALIBUR
30737 KING UTHER
30738 KING PELLINORE
30739 KING LEODEGRANCE
30740 MERLIN
30741 JOYOUS GARD
30742 CAMELOT
30743 LYONNESSE
30744 MAID OF ASTOLAT
30745 TINTAGEL
30746 PENDRAGON
30747 ELAINE
30748 VIVIEN
30749 ISEULT
30750 MORGAN LE FAY

30751 ETARRE
30752 LINETTE
30753 MELISANDE
30754 THE GREEN KNIGHT
30755 THE RED KNIGHT

'SCOTCH' ARTHURS

30763 SIR BORS DE GANIS
30764 SIR GAWAIN
30765 SIR GARETH
30766 SIR GERAINT
30767 SIR VALENCE
30768 SIR BALIN
30769 SIR BALAN
30770 SIR PRIANIUS
30771 SIR SAGRAMORE
30772 SIR PERCIVALE
30773 SIR LAVAINE
30774 SIR GAHERIS
30775 SIR AGRAVAINE
30776 SIR GALAGARS
30777 SIR LAMIEL
30778 SIR PELLEAS
30779 SIR COLGREVANCE
30780 SIR PERSANT
30781 SIR AGLOVALE
30782 SIR BRIAN
30783 SIR GILLEMERE

30784 SIR NEROVENS
30785 SIR MADOR DE LA PORTE
30786 SIR LIONEL
30787 SIR MENADEUKE
30788 SIR URRE OF THE MOUNT
30789 SIR GUY
30790 SIR VILLIARS
30791 SIR UWAINE
30792 SIR HERVIS DE REVEL

'EASTLEIGH' ARTHURS
(with six-wheel tenders)

30793 SIR ONTZLAKE
30794 SIR ECTOR DE MARIS
30795 SIR DINADAN
30796 SIR DODINAS LE SAVAGE
30797 SIR BLAMOR DE GANIS
30798 SIR HECTIMERE
30799 SIR IRONSIDE
30800 SIR MELEAUS DE LILE
30801 SIR MELIOT DE LOGRES
30802 SIR DURNORE
30803 SIR HARRY LE FISE LAKE
30804 SIR CADOR OF CORNWALL
30805 SIR CONSTANTINE
30806 SIR GALLERON

No.30737

No.30745

Photos: R.C. Riley

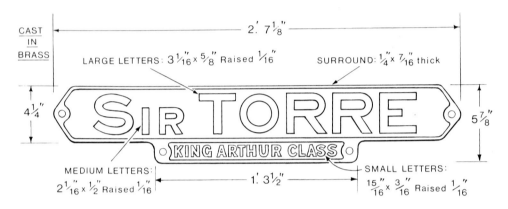

No.30782. One of the Scottish-built Arthurs which had different shaped letters in the appendage below the name. *C.L. Caddy*

CAST IN BRASS

2' 7⅛"

LARGE LETTERS: $3\frac{1}{16}" \times \frac{5}{8}"$ Raised $\frac{1}{16}"$

SURROUND: $\frac{1}{4}" \times 7\frac{1}{16}"$ thick

4¼"

5⅞"

MEDIUM LETTERS: $2\frac{1}{16}" \times \frac{1}{2}"$ Raised $\frac{1}{16}"$

1' 3½"

SMALL LETTERS: $\frac{15}{16}" \times \frac{3}{16}"$ Raised $\frac{1}{16}"$

Note: S.R. No's 736 to 754 had black backgrounds to their nameplates when first fitted. All others were painted in poppy red, but subsequently, British Railways repainted many of the Southern nameplates black when applying their own livery.

No.30795

L.M. Hobdey

No.30798

J. Oatway

Left: 'Urie' Arthur No.30755 THE RED KNIGHT in shining B.R. livery at Boscombe Station in October, 1949. This was one of eight in the class to receive a large chimney and two of these were also fitted with additional spark arresters.

G.O.P. Pearce

Above: No.30785   *J. Oatway*

Above: 30788   *A.G. Williamson by courtesy of R.C. Riley*

Below: No.30803   *J. Oatway*

'LORD NELSON' CLASS

Above: No.850 (later B.R. No. 30850) as built with a small chimney and tender.
British Rail

The first of this 4-6-0 class appeared in August, 1926, and it was not until two years later that more were completed. Sixteen were in service by the end of 1929.

30850 LORD NELSON
30851 Sir FRANCIS DRAKE
30852 Sir WALTER RALEIGH
30853 Sir RICHARD GRENVILLE
30854 HOWARD of EFFINGHAM
30855 ROBERT BLAKE
30856 LORD St VINCENT
30857 LORD HOWE
30858 LORD DUNCAN
30859 LORD HOOD
30860 LORD HAWKE
30861 LORD ANSON
30862 LORD COLLINGWOOD
30863 LORD RODNEY
30864 Sir MARTIN FROBISHER
30865 Sir JOHN HAWKINS

Above: No.857 (later B.R. No. 30857) as rebuilt in 1936 with an experimental boiler and re-shaped smoke deflectors.
Designer, Mr. R.E.L. Maunsell, was proposing to introduce a Pacific design, and it was the intention to use such a boiler for this. *British Rail*

Left: No.30854 in B.R. green livery shows the class in its final form with high-sided tender, smoke deflectors and large diameter chimney. The latter was fitted in 1939, and clearly improved steaming.
Photomatic

This class was named entirely after famous British Admirals and Captains, and as with **REMEMBRANCE** and **KING ARTHUR**, the nameplate on the left did not display the class after which it was named.

Above: No.30850

R.C. Riley

Right: No.30851
G.O.P. Pearce

No.30852

No.30853

These four photographs are by J. Oatway

No.30854. This one should have been preceded with 'LORD' but was omitted owing to its length.

No.30855. Appointed by Cromwell as a General-at-Sea, ROBERT BLAKE did not have a title as did the other Admirals of the class.

Below: No.30861. This, and No.30862, survived until October 6th, 1962.

C.L. Caddy

No.30862.   *C.L. Caddy*

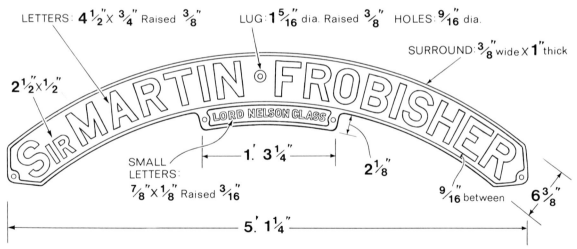

LETTERS: **4**$\frac{1}{2}$**″ X** $\frac{3}{4}$**″** Raised $\frac{3}{8}$**″**   LUG: **1**$\frac{5}{16}$**″** dia. Raised $\frac{3}{8}$**″**   HOLES: $\frac{9}{16}$**″** dia.

SURROUND: $\frac{3}{8}$**″** wide X **1″** thick

2$\frac{1}{2}$**″ X** $\frac{1}{2}$**″**

SMALL
LETTERS:
$\frac{7}{8}$**″ X** $\frac{1}{8}$**″** Raised $\frac{3}{16}$**″**

1.′ 3$\frac{1}{4}$**″**

2$\frac{1}{8}$**″**

$\frac{9}{16}$**″** between   **6**$\frac{3}{8}$**″**

5.′ 1$\frac{1}{4}$**″**

*Note: Although originally painted with poppy red backgrounds, during the later
B R. days the nameplates appeared in black.*

No.30856   *J. Oatway*

No.30857   *C.L. Caddy*

57

These 4-4-0 type engines, officially called Class 'V', were all named after public schools, and were the most powerful locomotives of their type in the country.
Introduced in 1930, they were built in various groups up to 1935. The last twenty were withdrawn late in 1962.

Above: The first of the class, as originally built in March, 1930.
British Rail

Left: One of the final batch to appear with smoke deflectors and larger cab windows.
Lens of Sutton

'SCHOOLS' CLASS

30900 ETON	30910 MERCHANT TAYLORS	30920 RUGBY	30929 MALVERN
30901 WINCHESTER	30911 DOVER	30921 SHREWSBURY	30930 RADLEY
30902 WELLINGTON	30912 DOWNSIDE	30922 MARLBOROUGH	30931 KING'S-WIMBLEDON
30903 CHARTERHOUSE	30913 CHRIST'S HOSPITAL	30923 UPPINGHAM/	30932 BLUNDELL'S
30904 LANCING	30914 EASTBOURNE	BRADFIELD	30933 KING'S-CANTERBURY
30905 TONBRIDGE	30915 BRIGHTON	30924 HAILEYBURY	30934 ST. LAWRENCE
30906 SHERBORNE	30916 WHITGIFT	30925 CHELTENHAM	30935 SEVENOAKS
30907 DULWICH	30917 ARDINGLY	30926 REPTON	30936 CRANLEIGH
30908 WESTMINSTER	30918 HURSTPIERPOINT	30927 CLIFTON	30937 EPSOM
30909 ST. PAUL'S	30919 HARROW	30928 STOWE	30938 ST OLAVE'S
			30939 LEATHERHEAD

Right: No.30919 and twenty others in the class were fitted with the wide Lemaitre chimney for multiple-jet blastpipe. The S.R. began fitting these in 1938 in an effort to improve the steaming, not that the 'Schools' were poor performers!
Lens of Sutton

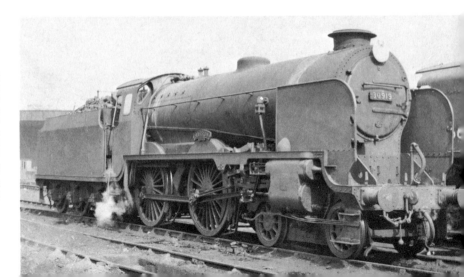

No.30903   *C.L. Caddy*

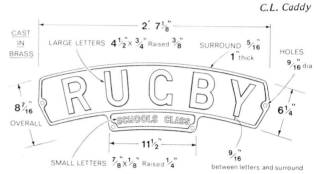

No.30934   *C.L. Caddy*

Below: No.30921   *G.O.P. Pearce*

As with the other Southern nameplates, the 'Schools' class plates were cast in various lengths. The shortest took up to 8 letters, the medium-sized 9 to 12, and the longest 13 or more.

However, the medium-sized nameplates fitted to No.30938, *above*, had only 8 letters! The '**T**' was also high and without a full stop.   *F.B.*

No.30926   *British Rail*

Below: No.30931   *J. Oatway*

S.R. No.21C1 (later B.R. No.35001) CHANNEL PACKET as it first appeared in 1941.

British Rail Photos

'MERCHANT NAVY' CLASS

The first of this revolutionary class appeared in 1941 during the height of the war, and the last ones, with modifications were not completed until 1949. In 1956, the first rebuild emerged *as below*.
The air-smoothed casing had gone and Walschaerts valve gear replaced the troublesome chain-driven gear.

35001 CHANNEL PACKET
35002 UNION CASTLE
35003 ROYAL MAIL
35004 CUNARD WHITE STAR
35005 CANADIAN PACIFIC
35006 PENINSULAR & ORIENTAL S.N.CO.
35007 ABERDEEN COMMONWEALTH
35008 ORIENT LINE
35009 SHAW SAVILL
35010 BLUE STAR
35011 GENERAL STEAM NAVIGATION

35012 UNITED STATES LINES
35013 BLUE FUNNEL LINE/
BLUE FUNNEL
CERTUM PETE FINEM
35014 NEDERLAND LINE
35015 ROTTERDAM LLOYD
35016 ELDERS FYFFES
35017 BELGIAN MARINE
35018 BRITISH INDIA LINE
35019 *French Line* C.G.T.

35020 BIBBY LINE
35021 NEW ZEALAND LINE
35022 HOLLAND AMERICA LINE
35023 HOLLAND-AFRIKA LINE
35024 EAST ASIATIC COMPANY
35025 BROCKLEBANK LINE
35026 LAMPORT & HOLT LINE
35027 PORT LINE
35028 CLAN LINE
35029 ELLERMAN LINES
35030 ELDER-DEMPSTER LINES

Below: No.35018 BRITISH INDIA LINE, first to be rebuilt in February, 1956. Eventually, the whole class was modified.

The nameplates, too, were revolutionary. They carried the names of shipping companies, many of which used the Southern Railway docks. The centrepiece, finished in vitreous enamel, displayed the house-flag of each line, which, in the majority of cases, flew towards the rear of the locomotive.

As shown on the right, most of the class first went into service with their nameplates boarded-up until a suitable time could be arranged for a naming ceremony.   *F.B.*

S.R. No.21C1 (later B.R. No.35001) as it first appeared in Southern livery. *G.O.P. Pearce*

S.R. No.21C9 (later B.R. No.35009) in wartime black livery.

No.21C6 (later B.R. No.35006). First to have the smaller 3in. high letters as compared with $4^5/_8$in. letters which eight of the first batch displayed. This was also one of three in the class to have its flag flying in the same direction on both sides.

British Rail Photos

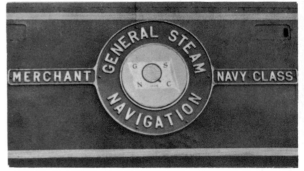

S.R. No.21C10 (later B.R. No.35010)

S.R. No.21C11 (later B.R. No.35011). The only nameplate to have "STEAM" in the title.

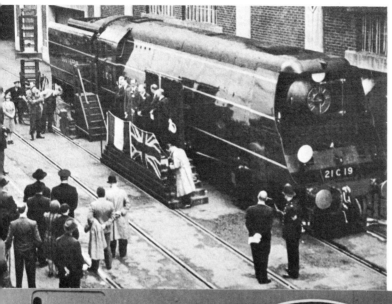

THE FRENCH CONNECTION

The occasion was Saturday, 22nd September, 1945, and the location: Southampton Docks.

In the shadow of the great French liner *Ile de France*, which had just been handed back after having been seized at Singapore in 1940, the 19th locomotive of the 'Merchant Navy' class was appropriately named *French Line* C.G.T.

The photograph shows the scene shortly before the unveiling of the nameplate by M. de Malglaive, Director of the French Line.

The above was the only nameplate to have script lettering. This was used by French Line in their publicity matter.

THE NAMING OF No. 35025

The time is four years later, 20th September, 1949, and the place: Waterloo Station, scene of so many naming ceremonies. Mr. S.W. Smart, OBE., Superintendent of Operation, Southern Region, together with Mr. R.P. Biddle, CBE., Docks and Marine Manager, preside at the ceremony whilst Col. Denis H. Bates, MC., TD., Chairman of the Shipping Company performs the unveiling of the nameplate.

British Rail Photos

MODIFICATIONS TO 'MERCHANT NAVY' NAMEPLATES

Two locomotives of the class had their nameplates changed after being in service. One of these was No.21C13 (later B.R. No.35013) which was originally named BLUE FUNNEL LINE at Waterloo Station on April 17th, 1945. By July of that year, however, new plates had been fitted. In place of the word "LINE" a latin phrase, meaning "make a good job of it", was substituted.
Another change involved No.35012. Named at Waterloo Station on April 10th, 1945, it was given a full house-flag in 1951.

British Rail Photos

Right:
No.35012 as revised with full house-flag. It was the same on both sides.

D.H. Cape

No.35018 after modification showing the nameplate fitted to the sides of the boiler in approximately the same position as on the previous 'air-smoothed' casing.

C.P. Boocock

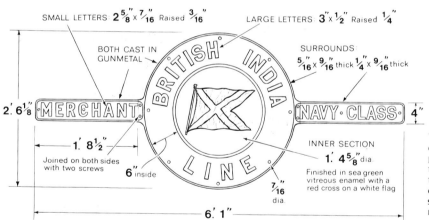

SMALL LETTERS $2\frac{5}{8}"$ x $\frac{7}{16}"$ Raised $\frac{3}{16}"$

LARGE LETTERS: $3"$ x $\frac{1}{2}"$ Raised $\frac{1}{4}"$

BOTH CAST IN GUNMETAL

SURROUNDS: $\frac{5}{16}"$ x $\frac{9}{16}"$ thick $\frac{1}{4}"$ x $\frac{9}{16}"$ thick

$2'\,6\frac{1}{8}"$

$1'\,8\frac{1}{2}"$

Joined on both sides with two screws

$6"$ inside

$4"$

INNER SECTION $1'\,4\frac{5}{8}"$ dia

Finished in sea green vitreous enamel with a red cross on a white flag

$\frac{7}{16}"$ dia.

$6'\,1"$

Originally, the background colour of these plates was red, but during B.R. days many were repainted black.

When the 'Merchant Navy' class was rebuilt the nameplates were transferred from the 'air-smoothed' casing to the boiler sides, and because of the curvature, a special supporting cradle had to be made. This measured: $9\frac{1}{2}$in. deep at the base tapering to $1\frac{1}{4}$in. at the top.

Left: No.35007 had the distinction of being the only nameplate with $3\frac{5}{8}$in. letters.

C.L. Caddy

S.R. No.21C116 BODMIN (later B.R. No.34016) as built in November, 1945.   *British Rail*

After the advent of the 'Merchant Navy' class, there was a need for a lighter version to operate over many of the restricted routes. Thus a new class was born. Known generally, as 'Lightweight Pacifics', a total of sixty-six were built between 1945 and 1950. From 1957, forty-three of the class were modified as below.

No.34102 LAPFORD, one of the last batch to be built in 1950, shows the re-designed tender which allowed better vision when running in reverse.   *T. Boustead*

'WEST COUNTRY' CLASS

Below: No.34004 YEOVIL as rebuilt in 1958.   *British Rail*

ILFRACOMBE

WEST COUNTRY CLASS

Above: S.R. No.21C117 (later B.R. No.34017) as first fitted. When modified the nameplate and shield were reversed *as shown on the right.* Each of the class was named after a place in the West Country where most of them saw service. *British Rail Photos*

ILFRACOMBE

WEST COUNTRY CLASS

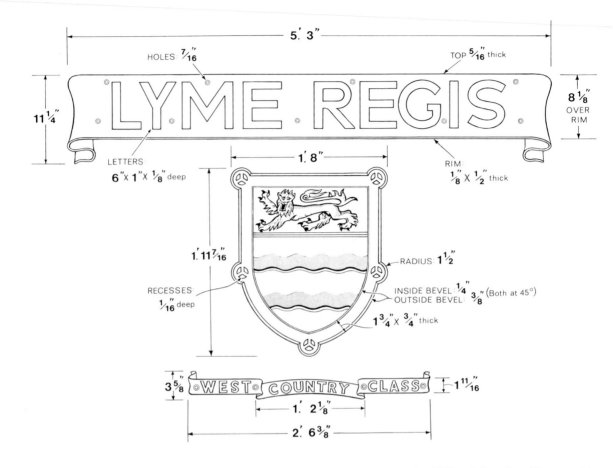

The distance between the top plate and shield was generally 4in. with 3in. between the shield and class plate. The nameplate and shield surround were made of gunmetal with the shield insert cut from mild steel and finished in vitreous enamel. The above shield had a beige coloured lion on a red ground with white and blue waves below. The background colour of the plates was red, although some were painted black in B.R. days.

34001 EXETER*	34024 TAMAR VALLEY	34047 CALLINGTON
34002 SALISBURY*	34025 ROUGH TOR/	34048 CREDITON*
34003 PLYMOUTH*	WHIMPLE	34091 WEYMOUTH*
34004 YEOVIL*	34026 YES TOR	34092 WELLS*/ CITY OF WELLS*
34005 BARNSTAPLE*	34027 TAW VALLEY	34093 SAUNTON
34006 BUDE*	34028 EDDYSTONE	34094 MORTEHOE
34007 WADEBRIDGE*	34029 LUNDY	34095 BRENTOR
34008 PADSTOW*	34030 WATERSMEET	34096 TREVONE
34009 LYME REGIS*	34031 TORRINGTON*	34097 HOLSWORTHY
34010 SIDMOUTH*	34032 CAMELFORD	34098 TEMPLECOMBE
34011 TAVISTOCK*	34033 CHARD	34099 LYNMOUTH
34012 LAUNCESTON*	34034 HONITON*	34100 APPLEDORE
34013 OKEHAMPTON*	34035 SHAFTESBURY	34101 HARTLAND
34014 BUDLEIGH SALTERTON*	34036 WESTWARD HO	34102 LAPFORD
34015 EXMOUTH*	34037 CLOVELLY	34103 CALSTOCK
34016 BODMIN*	34038 LYNTON	34104 BERE ALSTON
34017 ILFRACOMBE*	34039 BOSCASTLE	34105 SWANAGE
34018 AXMINSTER*	34040 CREWKERNE*	34106 LYDFORD
34019 BIDEFORD*	34041 WILTON	34107 BLANDFORD*/
34020 SEATON*	34042 DORCHESTER*	BLANDFORD FORUM*
34021 DARTMOOR*	34043 COMBE MARTIN	34108 WINCANTON
34022 EXMOOR	34044 WOOLACOMBE	
34023 BLACKMOOR VALE/	34045 OTTERY ST. MARY	
BLACKMORE VALE	34046 BRAUNTON	

By the time these locomotives were officially named they were carrying shields.

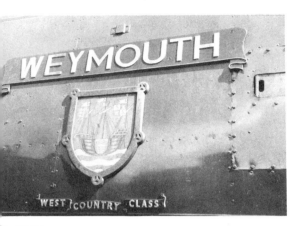

No.34091   *C.L. Caddy*

No.34023. The distance between the plates was approx. 12in. at the centre point.   *J. Oatway*

No.34006, shortest name in the class, it carried a Cornwall coat of arms originally.   *J. Oatway*

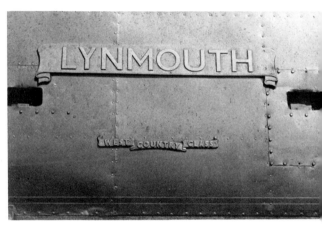

No.34099. The distance between the plates here was approx. 18in. at the centre point.   *D.H. Cape*

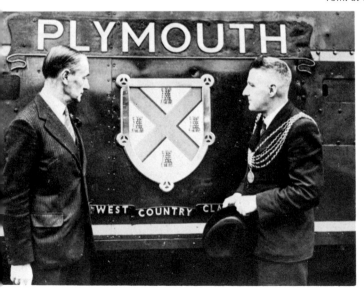

Naming ceremonies were held for a number of the 'West Country' class. Here we see the locomotive's Designer, Mr. O.V.S. Bulleid, *left*, with the Lord Mayor, Alderman Mason after the unveiling of PLYMOUTH at Plymouth Friary Station on July 11th, 1945.   *British Rail*

Those locomotives without shields generally had the class scroll fitted closer to the nameplate, but on some, like CHARD, the space was much greater suggesting that a shield was intended.   *C.L. Caddy*

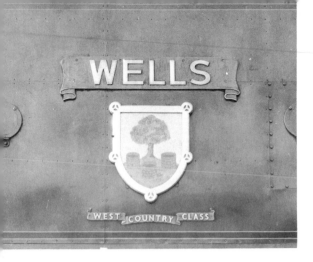

MODIFICATIONS TO 'WEST COUNTRY' NAMEPLATES

This class, too, had some name changes. No.34092 WELLS first named in November, 1949, had its nameplate replaced by a much longer one, CITY OF WELLS in March, 1950. Another alteration affected No.34023 where the name was spelt incorrectly. No.34025 was named ROUGH TOR for a few days in 1948. No.34006 BUDE, and No.34015 EXMOUTH, both had their county shields changed for town coat of arms.

Photos:
above and below
British Rail

Left:
G.O.P. Pearce

Another major change to No.34107 BLANDFORD which was changed in October, 1952 to BLANDFORD FORUM.
Being a shorter double-line plate, traces of the previous nameplate's position could still be seen!

No.34031 as it appeared in 1949.

No.34031 as modified in November, 1958.

BEFORE AND AFTER

The matched photographs, *above and top right*, of No.34031 show the relative positions of the nameplates on the original 'air-smoothed' casing, and later, on the special backplate that stood on the running board of the modified locomotive.

Below is another pair of scaled pictures showing No.34095 BRENTOR which had no shield. On the original version, the class scroll was fitted 12in. below the plate, but on the rebuilt engine they were fitted closer together.

Above: No.34014. One of three nameplates to have two lines. The height of the letters was 3in. instead of the usual 6in.

British Rail Photos except where stated

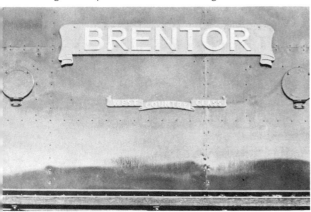

Above: No.34095 as first fitted.

Below: No.34045 with 5in. high letters.   *D.H. Cape*

Above: No.34095 as modified.   *D.H. Cape*

Below: No.34036 without the exclamation mark !   *J. Oatway*

S.R. No.21C167 (later B.R. No.34067) TANGMERE as built and resplendent in malachite green, September, 1947.

'BATTLE OF BRITAIN' CLASS

Basically, this class of forty-four locomotives was of the same design as the previous class, but because they were introduced later, in December, 1946, they included a number of modifications, such as the forward cab window design and longer smoke deflectors. These were eventually incorporated on some of the earlier Bulleid Pacifics.

Below: No.34087 **145 SQUADRON** as rebuilt in December, 1960. A total of seventeen were modified.

This new class was given appropriate names because many of the squadrons operated within the Southern Railway territory. Each of the locomotives, except No.34110 66 SQUADRON, carried an oval plaque with either its own badge or the R.A.F. insignia.

The *above* picture shows 615 SQUADRON as first fitted to No.34071. Later, they were transferred to No.34082.

British Rail Photos

THREE BY THREE THEY CAME TO BE CHRISTENED

It was on the seventh anniversary of the Battle of Britain that a number of the Bulleid Pacifics were officially named to commemorate the great event. The first three engines WINSTON CHURCHILL, LORD DOWDING and FIGHTER COMMAND, literally queued up for the honour!

It was Platform 11 of Waterloo Station on September 11th, 1947. A grand occasion with a guard of R.A.F. personnel, and also the R.A.F. Band. *Above:* Lord Dowding, Marshal of the Royal Air Force, unveils the nameplate of the first locomotive WINSTON CHURCHILL, saying he wished the great war-time leader could have been there in person.

A few days later, on September 16th, and again at Waterloo Station, three more were named: LORD BEAVERBROOK, HURRICANE and SPITFIRE. *Left:* Lord Beaverbrook, who was Minister of Aircraft Production during the Battle unveils his own nameplate and coat of arms.

At Brighton Station on September 19th three more locomotives were christened: SIR KEITH PARK, FIGHTER PILOT and TANGMERE.

British Rail Photos

34049	ANTI-AIRCRAFT COMMAND	34065	HURRICANE	34079	141 SQUADRON
34050	ROYAL OBSERVER CORPS	34066	SPITFIRE	34080	74 SQUADRON
34051	WINSTON CHURCHILL	34067	TANGMERE	34081	92 SQUADRON
34052	LORD DOWDING	34068	KENLEY	34082	615 SQUADRON
34053	SIR KEITH PARK	34069	HAWKINGE	34083	605 SQUADRON
34054	LORD BEAVERBROOK	34070	MANSTON	34084	253 SQUADRON
34055	FIGHTER PILOT	34071	615 SQUADRON/	34085	501 SQUADRON
34056	CROYDON		601 SQUADRON	34086	219 SQUADRON
34057	BIGGIN HILL	34072	257 SQUADRON	34087	145 SQUADRON
34058	SIR FREDERICK PILE	34073	249 SQUADRON	34088	213 SQUADRON
34059	SIR ARCHIBALD SINCLAIR	34074	46 SQUADRON	34089	602 SQUADRON
34060	25 SQUADRON	34075	264 SQUADRON	34090	SIR EUSTACE MISSENDEN SOUTHERN RAILWAY
34061	73 SQUADRON	34076	41 SQUADRON		
34062	17 SQUADRON	34077	603 SQUADRON	34109	SIR TRAFFORD LEIGH MALLORY
34063	229 SQUADRON	34078	222 SQUADRON	34110	66 SQUADRON
34064	FIGHTER COMMAND				

Note: The oval plaque fitted to the above locomotives depicted either the R.A.F. insignia, a squadron badge or a personal coat of arms. No.34110 however, is reported not to have carried a plaque.

'ALL CHANGE'
FOR TWO PLAQUES

Left: J. Oatway   *Above: M.R. Thresh*

An unfortunate mistake occurred in September 1960, when two locomotives, No.34058 SIR FREDERICK PILE and No.34068 KENLEY, were undergoing overhaul at Eastleigh Works. The nameplates and badges had been removed and when they were re-fitted the oval plaques were unfortunately changed over. The coat of arms was originally with No.34058 and the R.A.F. insignia with No.34068. It is understood that both locomotives, *as shown above*, ran with the wrong plaques until they were withdrawn from service.

A SELECTION OF NAMEPLATES WITH THE R.A.F. INSIGNIA

No.34057
C.L. Caddy

No.34065   *British Rail*

No.34066   *British Rail*

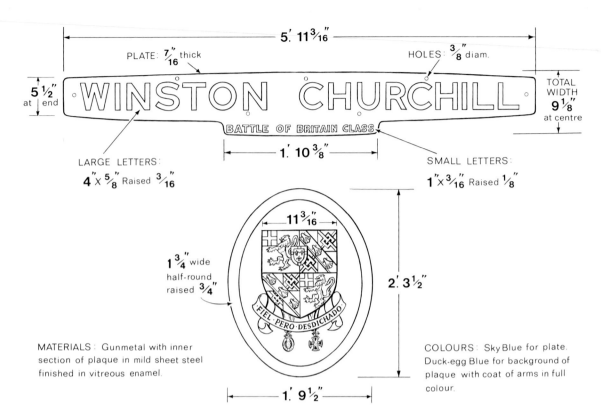

5' 11³⁄₁₆"

PLATE: ⁷⁄₁₆" thick

HOLES: ³⁄₈" diam.

WINSTON CHURCHILL

BATTLE OF BRITAIN CLASS

5½" at end

TOTAL WIDTH 9⅛" at centre

1' 10³⁄₈"

LARGE LETTERS:
4" x ⁵⁄₈" Raised ³⁄₁₆"

SMALL LETTERS:
1" x ³⁄₁₆" Raised ⅛"

11³⁄₁₆"

1³⁄₄" wide
half-round
raised ³⁄₄"

FIEL · PERO · DESDICHADO

2' 3½"

MATERIALS: Gunmetal with inner
section of plaque in mild sheet steel
finished in vitreous enamel.

COLOURS: Sky Blue for plate.
Duck-egg Blue for background of
plaque with coat of arms in full
colour.

1' 9½"

The distance between the nameplate and oval plaque was approx. 7½in. but for those of the class on
the 'Golden Arrow' duty, the plaque was lowered another 6in. to allow the Arrow to be fitted
in between.

Below: No.34109. The longest nameplate in the class, 7ft. long with 3in. high letters.   G.O.P. Pearce

No.34089. As with the 'West Country' class, the nameplate and badge were reversed after rebuilding.   *R.A. Cover*

J. Oatway

Two locomotives of the 'Battle of Britain' class, No.34050 *above* and No.34067 TANGMERE *right*, were both presented with additional plaques which were fitted to the cabsides as illustrated. The one on No.34050 is the Long Service Medal Ribbon.

Top picture: R.A. Cover   *Below: N.E. Preedy*

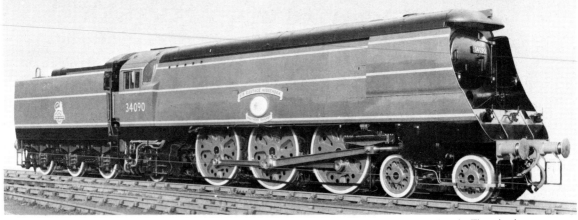

No.34090 in February, 1949. It had a special livery of Southern malachite green with yellow bands. The wheels were green with yellow tyres instead of black. *British Rail*

A FINAL TRIBUTE TO THE SOUTHERN RAILWAY

Of all the naming ceremonies which had taken place at Waterloo Station and elsewhere, none aroused greater interest than that on February 15th, 1949 when No.34090 was named.

It was a tribute not only to Sir Eustace, who was General Manager of the Southern Railway throughout the war, but also to the 67,000 employees who gave long hours of devoted service, particularly during the Battle of Britain, when the Railway's system was persistently attacked by enemy aircraft.

During its later life as an 'air-smoothed' locomotive, the livery was sadly changed to the usual B.R. colours. Even the two plates and oval plaque, which carried the Southern Railway coat of arms, were spaced out.
Mr. T. Boustead's photograph on the left confirms this.

The closer, more pleasing arrangement was re-adopted when the locomotive was modified, as below, in 1960.

British Rail

The length of the top plate was 5ft. 3¼in. with 3in. high letters. The bottom plate measured 3ft. 2in. long with 2in. and 1in. letters. The centrepiece was 2ft. 3½in. wide; being a standard 'Battle of Britain' oval plaque turned on its side.

THE PRE-GROUPING PERIOD

When the London, Midland & Scottish Railway was formed in 1923, most of the nameplates were carried by the L. & N.W.R. as shown on these two pages.

The famous preserved locomotive LION was originally with the Liverpool & Manchester Railway. Built in 1838, she saw service as a goods engine. *British Rail*

A close-up of the facsimile nameplate fitted when LION was reconditioned about 1930. *L. Hanson*

The standard curved plates used by the L. & N.W.R. varied in length. Above is OWL, one of the shortest nameplates fitted. The locomotive was built in 1854.

1847 saw this huge single-wheel design built by the London & North Western Railway at Crewe. Its nameplate had sunken letters, which were adopted by this line for most of their named engines. *British Rail*

The L.M.S. inherited a number of narrow-gauge railway systems, and above is one of the L. & N.W.R. engines which ran in the Crewe Works area. Built June, 1865. *L. Hanson*

The Lancashire & Yorkshire Railway also had some 1ft. 6in gauge engines running at Horwich Works. These had short plates fitted to the dome. Built by Beyer Peacock in 1887. *C.L. Caddy*

Left: Two engines built in 1882 by the North Staffordshire Railway had names. The plates were of similar style to those used by the L. & N.W.R. but the lettering was not so bold. The other engine was named JOHN BRAMLEY MOORE.

A number of the Scottish railways absorbed into the L.M.S. in 1923 had named locomotives; the names being hand applied to the splashers. The one above was with the Highland Railway, built in 1899 by Dübs & Co. of Glasgow.

J.L. Stevenson

Another example of the curved nameplate with recessed letters filled with black wax. This time, the name extends over two splashers! GREATER BRITAIN was built in 1891.

The Leek & Manifold Valley Light Railway had two narrow-gauge engines carrying combined name, number and works plates. Both built in 1904; the other engine being No. 1 E.R. CALTHROP.

Photomatic

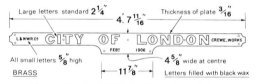

One of the L. & N.W.R. 'Precursor' class which was longer than usual.

One of the L. & N.W.R. 'Experiment' class.

Built in 1911, this celebrated engine of the 'George the Fifth' class, had special nameplates fitted.

L. Hanson

It was the practice of the L. & N.W.R. to select locomotives for the exclusive use of the various Engineering Departments. Their nameplates and numberplates were replaced by large cast plates on the cabsides. Many of them survived until L.M.S. days, and two of them are shown on the *right and below.*

Real Photos

Further special nameplates were carried by a 'Claughton' class engine when it appeared in 1920. *Photomatic*

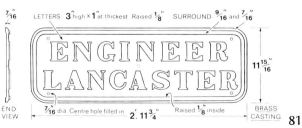

THE L.M.S. FROM 1923...

Above: The first of the class. Built in 1927, at the Queen's Park Works of the North British Locomotive Company of Glasgow.   *British Rail*

'ROYAL SCOT' CLASS

Few classes gained such fame as did the L.M.S. 'Royal Scots'. Unlike some of the major locomotives of other railways where only a few were built initially, the L.M.S. went ahead with the construction of fifty in the first year! Three years later, in 1930, another twenty were built.

Right: When L.M.S. No.6100 left for the North American Tour, she was fitted with an additional nameplate for the smoke-box door. Smoke deflectors were also fitted.   *Photomatic*

Below: From 1943, as the original locomotives became in need of heavy repair, they were rebuilt. Here we see the class in its final form.   *British Rail*

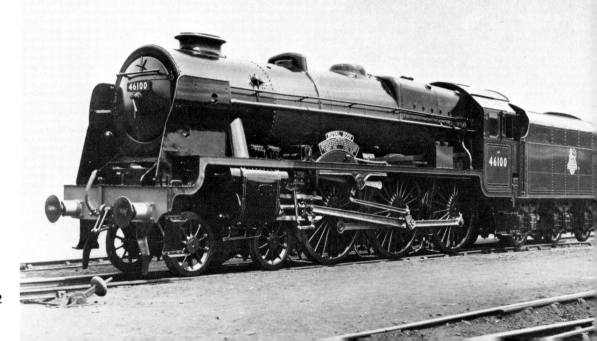

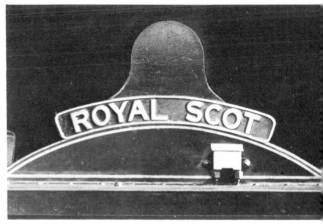

No nameplate had more changes than this one! When it first appeared in 1927, it was fitted above the wheel splasher by means of a supporting backplate. This was the method adopted for most L.M.S. named engines which did not carry a crest. However, in 1933, when it was decided to send one of the class to tour America and Canada, the number and name were permanently exchanged with those of L.M.S. No.6152. THE KING'S DRAGOON GUARDSMAN.

The nameplates were then fitted directly on top of the wheel splashers. The backplate seen above, suggests that a regimental crest was to have been fitted. It never materialised. On returning from the North American Tour, the locomotive received a large commemorative plaque instead. Then, when the locomotive was rebuilt in 1950, the words: "PRIOR TO CONVERSION" were added to the plaques. The "ROYAL SCOT" plates were replaced to line-up with the new radius.

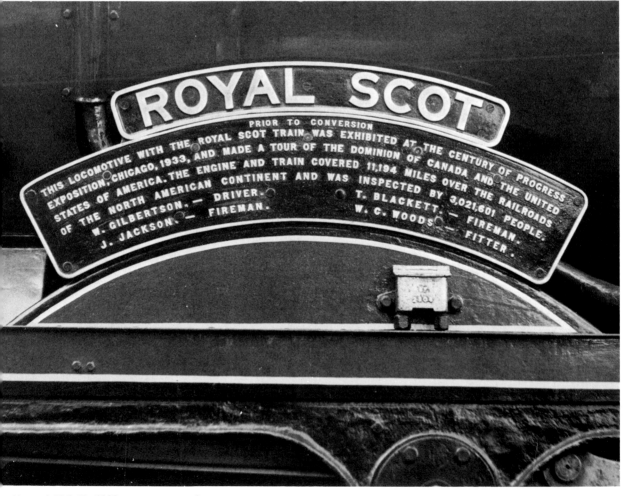

Above: L.M.S. No.6100 as now preserved.

D. Eatwell

46100 ROYAL SCOT	46137 VESTA°/
46101 ROYAL SCOTS GREY	THE PRINCE OF WALES'S VOLUNTEERS
46102 BLACK WATCH*	SOUTH LANCASHIRE*
46103 ROYAL SCOTS FUSILIER*	46138 FURY°/THE LONDON IRISH RIFLEMAN*
46104 SCOTTISH BORDERER	46139 AJAX°/THE WELCH REGIMENT*
46105 CAMERON HIGHLANDER	46140 HECTOR°/
46106 GORDON HIGHLANDER	THE KING'S ROYAL RIFLE CORPS
46107 ARGYLL AND SUTHERLAND HIGHLANDER*	46141 CALEDONIAN°/
46108 SEAFORTH HIGHLANDER	THE NORTH STAFFORDSHIRE REGIMENT*
46109 ROYAL ENGINEER*	46142 LION°/
46110 GRENADIER GUARDSMAN	THE YORK & LANCASTER REGIMENT
46111 ROYAL FUSILIER	46143 MAIL°/
46112 SHERWOOD FORESTER*	THE SOUTH STAFFORDSHIRE REGIMENT
46113 CAMERONIAN*	46144 OSTRICH°/HONOURABLE ARTILLERY COMPANY
46114 COLDSTREAM GUARDSMAN	46145 CONDOR°/THE DUKE OF WELLINGTON'S REGT.
46115 SCOTS GUARDSMAN	(WEST RIDING)*
46116 IRISH GUARDSMAN*	46146 JENNY LIND°/THE RIFLE BRIGADE*
46117 WELSH GUARDSMAN	46147 COURIER°/
46118 ROYAL WELCH FUSILIER*	THE NORTHAMPTONSHIRE REGIMENT*
46119 LANCASHIRE FUSILIER	46148 VELOCIPEDE°/THE MANCHESTER REGIMENT*
46120 ROYAL INNISKILLING FUSILIER*	46149 LADY OF THE LAKE°/
46121 H.L.I./HIGHLAND LIGHT INFANTRY	THE MIDDLESEX REGIMENT*
THE CITY OF GLASGOW REGIMENT*	46150 THE LIFE GUARDSMAN
46122 ROYAL ULSTER RIFLEMAN*	46151 THE ROYAL HORSE GUARDSMAN
46123 ROYAL IRISH FUSILIER*	46152 THE KING'S DRAGOON GUARDSMAN
46124 LONDON SCOTTISH*	46153 THE ROYAL DRAGOON
46125 LANCASHIRE WITCH°/3RD CARABINIER*	46154 THE HUSSAR
46126 SANSPAREIL°/ROYAL ARMY SERVICE CORPS*	46155 THE LANCER
46127 NOVELTY°/THE OLD CONTEMPTIBLE/	46156 THE SOUTH WALES BORDERER
OLD CONTEMPTIBLES 1914 AUG. 5 TO NOV. 22 ⊙	46157 THE ROYAL ARTILLERYMAN
46128 METEOR°/THE LOVAT SCOUTS*	46158 THE LOYAL REGIMENT*
46129 COMET°/THE SCOTTISH HORSE*	46159 THE ROYAL AIR FORCE
46130 LIVERPOOL°/	46160 QUEEN VICTORIA'S RIFLEMAN
THE WEST YORKSHIRE REGIMENT*	46161 THE KING'S OWN /KING'S OWN*
46131 PLANET°/	46162 QUEEN'S WESTMINSTER RIFLEMAN
THE ROYAL WARWICKSHIRE REGIMENT*	46163 CIVIL SERVICE RIFLEMAN
46132 PHOENIX°/	46164 THE ARTISTS' RIFLEMAN
THE KING'S REGIMENT LIVERPOOL*	46165 THE RANGER 12TH LONDON REGT.
46133 VULCAN°/THE GREEN HOWARDS*	46166 LONDON RIFLE BRIGADE*
46134 ATLAS°/THE CHESHIRE REGIMENT*	46167 THE HERTFORDSHIRE REGIMENT
46135 SAMSON°/	46168 THE GIRL GUIDE*
THE EAST LANCASHIRE REGIMENT*	46169 THE BOY SCOUT*
46136 GOLIATH°/THE BORDER REGIMENT*	46170 BRITISH LEGION ⊙

°*These carried an engraved oval brass plaque below the nameplate depicting the original locomotive.*

**At some time during their service these locomotives carried a regimental crest or badge.*

⊙*These nameplates were in the form of brass replica badges as below.*

Above: No.6170 (later 46170) actually was a 'one off' locomotive having been rebuilt in 1935 from the unsuccessful experimental engine No.6399 FURY. *Right:* A close-up of the nameplate as fitted to the forward splashers. It measured 21½in. wide by 22in. high. *Left:* Another 'badge' nameplate as fitted to L.M.S. No.6127. This measured 24½in. wide by 19⅞in. high.

British Rail Photos

No.46159. Most long names without crests were raised above the splasher with a supporting backplate.

British Rail

SINGLE
LINERS
WITHOUT
CRESTS

Above: An interesting picture of No.46155 which for a time carried rather large bolts. It was customary for the L.M.S. to use countersunk bolts flush with the background, and then paint over.

R.A. Cover

Below: No.46163. One of the few single-line plates without a crest to be fitted directly on top of the splasher.

British Rail

No.46102 with an elliptical crest fitted on the face of the splasher. *Real Photos*

SINGLE
LINERS
WITH
CRESTS

No.46118 had a trimmed circular crest which overlapped the backplate and splasher. *L. Hanson*

L.M.S. No.6127 before being renamed. It carried an oval brass plaque upon which was engraved: "NOVELTY" BUILT FOR THE LIVERPOOL & MANCHESTER RY IN 1829.
The above nameplate, and seven others named after early locomotives, were later transferred (without plaques) to 'Jubilee' class locomotives. *Real Photos*

L.M.S. No.6125. Another of the twenty-five originally named after early locomotives, that later made way for regiments.

Below: No.46103 which carried one of the largest and most impressive crests of the whole class. *L. Hanson*

No.46125 with the nameplate and crest which replaced the one illustrated *on the left*. *B. Hilton*

Below: No.46129. It was not usual to mount a nameplate and top crest with a supporting plate. *L. Hobdey*

SOME MEMORABLE 'ROYAL SCOT' NAMING CEREMONIES

Until the appearance of the 'Royal Scot' class, naming ceremonies of locomotives were almost unheard of. The L.M.S. went out of their way to make each one a grand affair, and from then on, other railway companies named their locomotives in a similar manner!

Above: A splendid gathering of military dignitaries including Lord Hampden and Lord Knutsford and also the Mayor of Watford witnessed the naming of L.M.S. No.6167 THE HERTFORDSHIRE REGIMENT at Watford Station on July 22nd, 1933.

Above and right: Central Press Photos

Above: A famous couple, Lord and Lady Baden-Powell name THE GIRL GUIDE (then L.M.S. No.6168) at Euston Station in December 1930. At the same time, they also named the next engine in the class: THE BOY SCOUT.

Left: British Rail

Below: C. Field

Above: A full military band was present at the naming of L.M.S. No.6112 SHERWOOD FORESTER at Derby on June 16th, 1933. On this occasion only engraved crests were fitted, but new ones, *as on the right*, were presented at Nottingham Station on September 18th, 1948.

This locomotive was often used to carry Battalions of the Regiment, and an engraved plate was fitted giving details.

DOUBLE LINERS *WITHOUT CRESTS*

No.46165 had an unusual nameplate with three sizes of lettering!

Originally L.M.S. No.6144 OSTRICH, this one w later presented with a crest.

No.46162. A "double liner" which never received a badge.   *All British Rail photos except where stated.*

DOUBLE LINERS *WITH CRESTS*

Above: No.46135

Below: No.46137. The last to be rebuilt in 1955. *L. Hanson*

Above: No.46130

Below: No.46145 Another plate with two sizes of lettering.

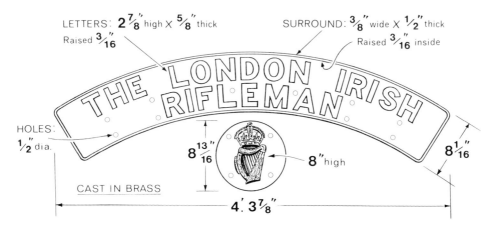

LETTERS: $2\frac{7}{8}''$ high X $\frac{5}{8}''$ thick
Raised $\frac{3}{16}''$

SURROUND: $\frac{3}{8}''$ wide X $\frac{1}{2}''$ thick
Raised $\frac{3}{16}''$ inside

HOLES: $\frac{1}{2}''$ dia.

$8\frac{13}{16}''$

$8''$high

$8\frac{1}{16}''$

CAST IN BRASS

$4'\ 3\frac{7}{8}''$

At first, the background colour of L.M.S. plates was black, but during the war and latter days of B.R. many were painted red.

o.46120

Real Photos

Left and Below:
An interesting variation if only temporary. Because of the position of the oil box on the left-hand side of L.M.S. No.6120, the oval crest was fitted so as to overlap the nameplate as below. It lasted only a short while however.

FROM THE SHORTEST TO THE LONGEST!

When built, L.M.S. No.6121 was named *as above* but on January 22nd, 1949, the locomotive officially received nameplates showing the full title, together with crest. With eight words, it became the longest name in the class.
C.L. Hodgetts

Above: One of the first two 'Patriots' to appear in 1930, rebuilt from the earlier 'Claughton' class. It was first numbered 5902, and for the official photograph had dummy nameplates! This locomotive finally became B.R. 45501 S^T DUNSTAN'S.

'PATRIOT' CLASS

Following the success of the 'Royal Scots', it was decided in 1930 to rebuild the 'Claughton' class with similar features, hence the reason why the 'Patriots' soon became known as the "Baby Scots". Eventually, a total of fifty-two were completed, ten of which never received names.

Eventually, the 'Patriots' were fitted with smoke deflectors in similar fashion to the 'Royal Scots'.   *British Rail Photos*

Below: When the above locomotive was renamed in 1937, the nameplates were transferred to L.M.S. No.5530. Here we see the locomotive, as rebuilt again in 1946. It became B.R. No.45530 and smoke deflectors were later fitted.

As with one of the earlier 'Claughtons', one of this class was given the honour of becoming the Memorial Engine. First of the class, L.M.S. No.5500 CROXTETH was renamed PATRIOT in 1937. It was then that the class became known as the 'Patriots'.

45500 CROXTETH/PATRIOT IN MEMORY OF THE FALLEN
        L.&.N.W.R. EMPLOYEES 1914–1919
45501 SIR FRANK REE/ST DUNSTAN'S ⊙
45502 ROYAL NAVAL DIVISION
45503 THE LEICESTERSHIRE REGIMENT*/
        THE ROYAL LEICESTERSHIRE REGIMENT*
45504 ROYAL SIGNALS*
45505 THE ROYAL ARMY ORDNANCE CORPS*
45506 THE ROYAL PIONEER CORPS*
45507 ROYAL TANK CORPS*
45508
45509 THE DERBYSHIRE YEOMANRY*
45510
45511 ISLE OF MAN*
45512 BUNSEN
45513
45514 HOLYHEAD
45515 CAERNARVON
45516 THE BEDFORDSHIRE AND
        HERTFORDSHIRE REGIMENT*
45517
45518 BRADSHAW
45519 LADY GODIVA
45520 LLANDUDNO*
45521 RHYL*
45522 PRESTATYN
45523 BANGOR
45524 SIR FREDERICK HARRISON/BLACKPOOL
45525 E. TOOTAL BROADHURST/COLWYN BAY*
45526 MORECAMBE AND HEYSHAM*
45527 SOUTHPORT*
45528 R.E.M.E.
45529 SIR HERBERT WALKER K.C.B./
        STEPHENSON
45530 SIR FRANK REE
45531 SIR FREDERICK HARRISON
45532 ILLUSTRIOUS
45533 LORD RATHMORE
45534 E. TOOTAL BROADHURST
45535 SIR HERBERT WALKER K.C.B.
45536 PRIVATE W. WOOD, V.C.
45537 PRIVATE E. SYKES V.C.
45538 GIGGLESWICK
45539 E.C. TRENCH
45540 SIR ROBERT TURNBULL
45541 DUKE OF SUTHERLAND
45542
45543 HOME GUARD
45544
45545 PLANET
45546 FLEETWOOD
45547
45548 LYTHAM ST. ANNES
45549
45550
45551

Above: L.M.S. No.5501 was also renamed in 1937 Sᵀ DUNSTAN'S
Photo: L. Hanson. Others: British Rail

No.45529

⊙ *This nameplate was in the form of brass replica badge.*

At some time during their service these locomotives carried a regimental crest or civic coat of arms.

No.45538

L.M.S. No.5511 as it first appeared without coat of arms.

No.45511 after being fitted with a coat of arms.

British Rail Photos except where stated.

No.45526

No.45521

Real Photos

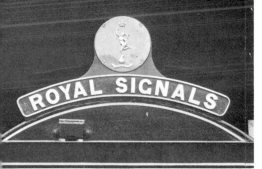

No.45504   *British Rail*

No.45541   *L. Hobdey*

No.45516, longest name in the class.   *B. Hilton*

MONTY NAMES A 'PATRIOT'

It was an auspicious occasion at Euston Station on September 15th, 1948 when the locomotive No.45506 was named **THE ROYAL PIONEER CORPS** by Field Marshal Viscount Montgomery.

This locomotive was one of a number of 'Patriots' which had run unnamed until late in their career. After the 'Royal Scots' had all been named, it was the turn of this class to accommodate the additional names.

Keystone Press Photo

No.45503 after "ROYAL" was added.   *British Rail*

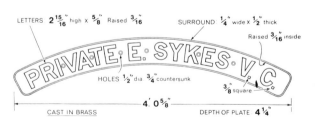

LETTERS 2$\frac{15}{16}$" high x $\frac{5}{8}$" Raised $\frac{3}{16}$"   SURROUND $\frac{1}{4}$" wide x $\frac{1}{2}$" thick   Raised $\frac{3}{16}$" inside

HOLES $\frac{1}{2}$" dia $\frac{3}{4}$" countersunk $\frac{3}{8}$" square

4' 0$\frac{5}{8}$"

CAST IN BRASS   DEPTH OF PLATE 4$\frac{1}{4}$"

No.45537 *above*, was one of the few L.M.S. nameplates without bolt holes at the ends. This was surprising in view of the long backplates to which these were usually fitted.

L.M.S. No.6201, second of the class to be built in 1933, showing the small tender and rather unsightly double chimney that was fitted in its early days.

'PRINCESS ROYAL' CLASS

In 1933, the first two L.M.S. Pacific 4-6-2's arrived on the scene, and two years later, eleven more were constructed with modifications. No doubt, more would have been built, but in 1937 the larger 'Coronation' class was introduced.

46200 THE PRINCESS ROYAL	46205 PRINCESS VICTORIA	46210 LADY PATRICIA
46201 PRINCESS ELIZABETH	46206 PRINCESS MARIE LOUISE	46211 QUEEN MAUD
46202 PRINCESS ANNE	46207 PRINCESS ARTHUR OF CONNAUGHT	46212 DUCHESS OF KENT
46203 PRINCESS MARGARET ROSE	46208 PRINCESS HELENA VICTORIA	
46204 PRINCESS LOUISE	46209 PRINCESS BEATRICE	

Below: The same locomotive with larger tender and more pleasing chimney as fitted later.   *British Rail Photos*

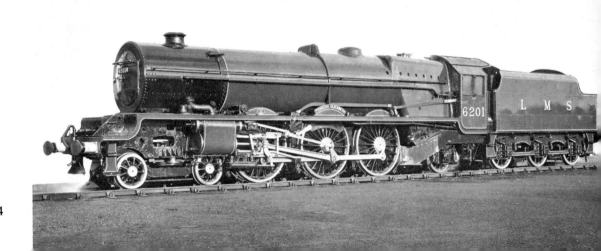

The nameplates of the 'Princess Royal' class were fitted above
the centre wheel splashers, with the exception of No.46202,
described on page 97. *Above* is No.46203, one of four in the class
to have impressive double-line nameplates.   *British Rail*

No.46200, first of the class.

R.C. Riley

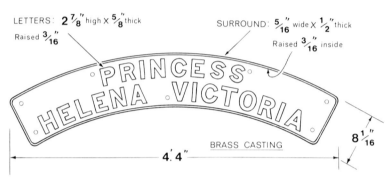

LETTERS: $2\frac{7}{8}''$ high X $\frac{5}{8}''$ thick

Raised $\frac{3}{16}''$

SURROUND: $\frac{5}{16}''$ wide X $\frac{1}{2}''$ thick

Raised $\frac{3}{16}''$ inside

PRINCESS HELENA VICTORIA

BRASS CASTING

$4'\ 4''$

$8\frac{1}{16}''$

Notes: Basically, the nameplates of this class had the same specifications as those of the 'Royal Scot' class without badges. All however, were fitted directly on top of the splasher, with the exception of the one described on the opposite page. According to the 1946 livery instructions they were to have had maroon backgrounds, but some were still seen to have black.

Fitting the nameplate at Crewe Works, July 28th, 1933.

Above: No.46206

British Rail Photos unless stated

Above: No.46210

B. Hilton

Below: No.46201

Right: No.46207

REBUILDING OF THE 'TURBOMOTIVE'

One of the class L.M.S. No.6202 was built in 1933 as an experimental turbine-driven locomotive. It did not carry a name at first, but was nicknamed "The Turbomotive". However, in 1952, it was rebuilt in similar fashion to the rest of the class, and named PRINCESS ANNE.
Unfortunately, shortly afterwards, it was involved in the tragic crash at Harrow and Wealdstone and was deemed irreparable.

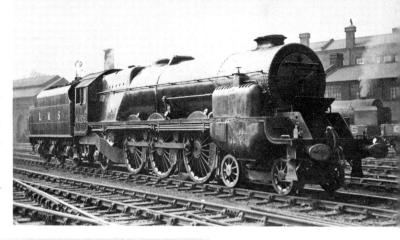

Above: The original L.M.S. Turbomotive at Camden.
Kelland Collection, courtesy Bournemouth Railway Club

Left: As rebuilt in 1952. The nameplates were positioned over the forward driving wheels.

Below: Fitting the nameplate. In the absence of a splasher, it had its own support.
British Rail

L.M.S. No.5158 (later B.R. No.45158)   GLASGOW YEOMANRY   *British Rail*

CLASS '5'

From 1934 until 1951, over 800 of these mixed-traffic locomotives were built. Yet, only a handful were actually named! They were highly successful, and were employed over almost every L.M.S. route. A number of modifications were made over the years, but they still retained their basic identity as a 'Black Five'.

45154 LANARKSHIRE YEOMANRY   45157 THE GLASGOW HIGHLANDER
45156 AYRSHIRE YEOMANRY   45158 GLASGOW YEOMANRY
       EARL OF CARRICK'S OWN   FIELD BRIGADE R.A.T.A.

Each of the above locomotives carried a regimental crest, and No's 45156 and 45158 had additional wording on small plates below the crests.

No.45154. The nameplates of this class were made at St. Rollox Works, Glasgow, and had lettering of a different style.   *D. Eatwe*

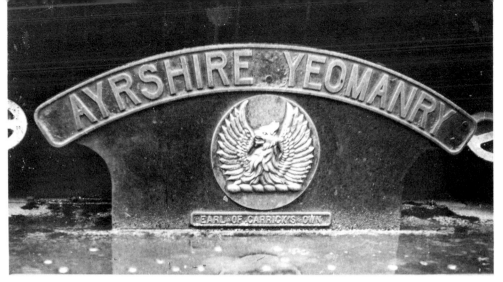

No.45156   *Real Photos*

Above: No.45157, the only one with a badge above the nameplate.

Below: No.45158. In the absence of splashers, the nameplates had their own supports.   *British Rail*

Above: L.M.S. No.5706 (later B.R. No.45706) shows the small tender which these engines at first received. They were transferred from the 'Royal Scots' when they in turn received high-sided tenders. This particular locomotive later carried a ship's badge below the nameplate. *British Rail*

'JUBILEE' CLASS

It was the intention that these engines, classified 5XP, should replace the earlier 'Patriots'. However, when they first took to the road in 1934, they were disappointing. There were obvious problems with steaming, and only after much modification did they 'find their feet'.

Altogether, 191 'Jubilees' were built, evidence enough, that the early difficulties were overcome.

Left: Several of the class were fitted for a time with double chimneys, and here we see BAHAMAS, now preserved in L.M.S. livery and numbered 5596.
T. Boustead

Right: B.R. No.45736 PHOENIX was one of two 'Jubilees' to be rebuilt in 1942. No.45735 COMET was the other locomotive. Later, similar rebuilding was carried out with the 'Royal Scot' and 'Patriot' classes.
B. Hilton

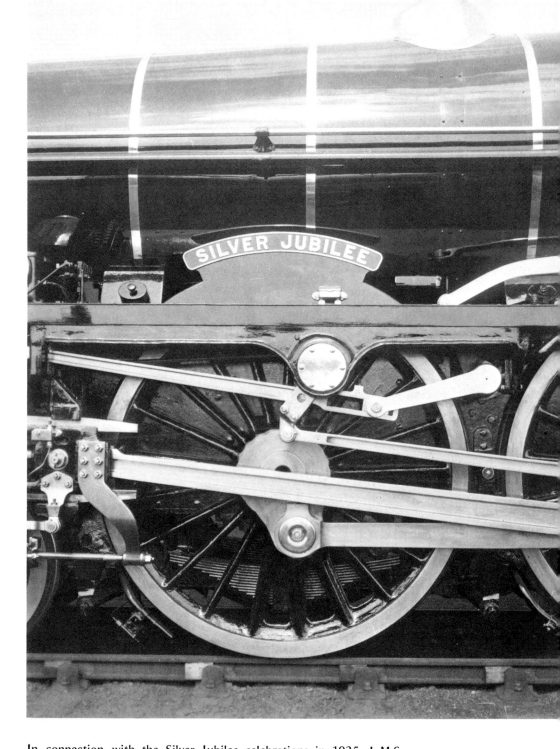

In connection with the Silver Jubilee celebrations in 1935, L.M.S. No.5642 was selected to appear at Euston Station in May of that year, with many parts, including the nameplates, finished in chrome. The locomotive actually exchanged its number with No.5552, and from then onwards, they became known as the 'Jubilees'. Most of the class received names either depicting places within the British Empire, or associated with the Royal Navy.   *British Rail*

45552 SILVER JUBILEE	45588 KASHMIR	45623 PALESTINE	45681 ABOUKIR
45553 CANADA	45589 GWALIOR	45624 St. HELENA	45682 TRAFALGAR
45554 ONTARIO	45590 TRAVANCORE	45625 SARAWAK	45683 HOGUE
45555 QUEBEC	45591 UDAIPUR	45626 SEYCHELLES	45684 JUTLAND
45556 NOVA SCOTIA	45592 INDORE	45627 SIERRA LEONE	45685 BARFLEUR
45557 NEW BRUNSWICK	45593 KOLHAPUR	45628 SOMALILAND	45686 St. VINCENT
45558 MANITOBA	45594 BHOPAL	45629 STRAITS	45687 NEPTUNE
45559 BRITISH COLUMBIA	45595 SOUTHERN	SETTLEMENTS	45688 POLYPHEMUS
45560 PRINCE EDWARD	RHODESIA*	45630 SWAZILAND	45689 AJAX⇔
ISLAND	45596 BAHAMAS	45631 TANGANYIKA	45690 LEANDER
45561 SASKATCHEWAN	45597 BARBADOS	45632 TONGA	45691 ORION
45562 ALBERTA	45598 BASUTOLAND	45633 TRANS-JORDAN/	45692 CYCLOPS
45563 AUSTRALIA	45599 BECHUANALAND	ADEN	45693 AGAMEMNON
45564 NEW SOUTH WALES	45600 BERMUDA	45634 TRINIDAD	45694 BELLEROPHON
45565 VICTORIA	45601 BRITISH GUIANA	45635 TOBAGO	45695 MINOTAUR
45566 QUEENSLAND	45602 BRITISH HONDURAS	45636 UGANDA	45696 ARETHUSA
45567 SOUTH AUSTRALIA	45603 SOLOMON ISLANDS	45637 WINDWARD	45697 ACHILLES
45568 WESTERN AUSTRALIA	45604 CEYLON	ISLANDS	45698 MARS
45569 TASMANIA	45605 CYPRUS	45638 ZANZIBAR	45699 GALATEA
45570 NEW ZEALAND	45606 FALKLAND ISLANDS	45639 RALEIGH	45700 BRITANNIA/
45571 SOUTH AFRICA	45607 FIJI	45640 FROBISHER	AMETHYST
45572 IRISH FREE STATE/	45608 GIBRALTAR	45641 SANDWICH	45701 CONQUEROR
EIRE	45609 GILBERT AND	45642 BOSCAWEN	45702 COLOSSUS
45573 NEWFOUNDLAND	ELLICE ISLANDS	45643 RODNEY	45703 THUNDERER
45574 INDIA	45610 GOLD COAST/	45644 HOWE	45704 LEVIATHAN
45575 MADRAS	GHANA	45645 COLLINGWOOD	45705 SEAHORSE
45576 BOMBAY	45611 HONG KONG	45646 NAPIER	45706 EXPRESS*
45577 BENGAL	45612 JAMAICA	45647 STURDEE	45707 VALIANT
45578 UNITED PROVINCES	45613 KENYA	45648 WEMYSS	45708 RESOLUTION
45579 PUNJAB	45614 LEEWARD ISLANDS	45649 HAWKINS	45709 IMPLACABLE
45580 BURMA	45615 MALAY STATES	45650 BLAKE	45710 IRRESISTIBLE
45581 BIHAR AND ORISSA	45616 MALTA/MALTA G.C.	45651 SHOVELL	45711 COURAGEOUS
45582 CENTRAL PROVINCES	45617 MAURITIUS	45652 HAWKE	45712 VICTORY
45583 ASSAM	45618 NEW HEBRIDES	45653 BARHAM	45713 RENOWN
45584 NORTH WEST	45619 NIGERIA	45654 HOOD	45714 REVENGE
FRONTIER	45620 NORTH BORNEO	45655 KEITH	45715 INVINCIBLE
45585 HYDERABAD	45621 NORTHERN	45656 COCHRANE	45716 SWIFTSURE
45586 MYSORE	RHODESIA	45657 TYRWHITT	45717 DAUNTLESS
45587 BARODA	45622 NYASALAND	45658 KEYES	45718 DREADNOUGHT
		45659 DRAKE	45719 GLORIOUS
		45660 ROOKE	45720 INDOMITABLE
		45661 VERNON	45721 IMPREGNABLE
		45662 KEMPENFELT	45722 DEFENCE
		45663 JERVIS	45723 FEARLESS
		45664 NELSON	45724 WARSPITE
		45665 LORD RUTHERFORD	45725 REPULSE
		OF NELSON	45726 VINDICTIVE
		45666 CORNWALLIS	45727 INFLEXIBLE
		45667 JELLICOE	45728 DEFIANCE
		45668 MADDEN	45729 FURIOUS
		45669 FISHER	45730 OCEAN
		45670 HOWARD OF	45731 PERSEVERANCE
		EFFINGHAM	45732 SANSPAREIL ⇔
		45671 PRINCE RUPERT	45733 NOVELTY⇔
		45672 ANSON	45734 METEOR ⇔
		45673 KEPPEL	45735 COMET⇔
		45674 DUNCAN	45736 PHOENIX⇔
		45675 HARDY	45737 ATLAS⇔
		45676 CODRINGTON	45738 SAMSON⇔
		45677 BEATTY	45739 ULSTER*
		45678 DE ROBECK	45740 MUNSTER
		45679 ARMADA	45741 LEINSTER
		45680 CAMPERDOWN	45742 CONNAUGHT

*At sometime during their service these locomotives carried a badge or coat of arms.

⇔These nameplates were transferred from 'Royal Scots' but without the oval brass plaques.

Left: As the finishing touches are applied to L.M.S. No.5739 ULSTER, at Crewe Works, fitters pass by with nameplates for the last three 'Jubilee' class locomotives, November 16th, 1936.

Fox Photos

No.45731

No.45667

No.45574

No.45735

The measurements shown on the right were standard for most of the short or medium length names. It is interesting to note however, that AJAX, COMET and ATLAS, three of the eight nameplates transferred from the 'Royal Scots', were actually shortened when fitted to the 'Jubilees'. This was due to the rather large space between the letters and ends of the original nameplates.

Another variation of this class was the different style of lettering used for plates cast at St. Rollox Works in Glasgow. *Three of these are shown on the right and below.*

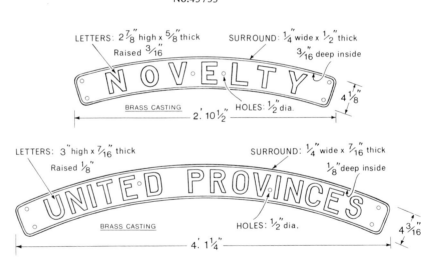

LETTERS: $2\frac{7}{8}$" high x $\frac{5}{8}$" thick
Raised $\frac{3}{16}$"

SURROUND: $\frac{1}{4}$" wide x $\frac{1}{2}$" thick
$\frac{3}{16}$" deep inside

BRASS CASTING

HOLES: $\frac{1}{2}$" dia.

$4\frac{1}{8}$"

2.' $10\frac{1}{2}$"

LETTERS: 3" high x $\frac{7}{16}$" thick
Raised $\frac{1}{8}$"

SURROUND: $\frac{1}{4}$" wide x $\frac{7}{16}$" thick
$\frac{1}{8}$" deep inside

BRASS CASTING

HOLES: $\frac{1}{2}$" dia.

$4\frac{3}{16}$"

4.' $1\frac{1}{4}$"

Below: No.45584. One of the long nameplates made at St. Rollox Works.

Below: No.45580. One of the short ones. *Photos B. Hilton*

No.45665 was one of two in the class to have double-line nameplates. Note the two sizes of lettering.

No.45609 taken from a ¾-viewpoint. This was the only other 'Jubilee' to have double-lined nameplates.

Photos by B. Hilton

Above: One of three 'Jubilee' nameplates to receive badges. In order to accommodate the large plaque, a special backplate was fitted to raise-up the nameplate. The locomotive, L.M.S. No.5706, in its original condition appears on Page 100. *British Rail*

No.45595 as fitted with a coat of arms. *C.L. Caddy*

No.45739 *British Rail*

A NEW NAME FOR "TRANS-JORDAN"

From time to time, as Countries changed their identities, it was considered necessary to present new nameplates for the engine in question, and such an occasion arose on September 4th, 1946 when 'Jubilee' class No.5633 (later B.R. No.45633) was re-christened ADEN. Lt. Col. Sir Bernard Reilly, former Governor, was there at Euston Station to perform the unveiling of the new nameplates.

BEFORE AND AFTER. The pictures, *above and on the right*, provide an interesting comparison of the nameplates carried by L.M.S. No.5633. It appears that the same backplate was used for ADEN, which did not quite fit at the ends!

British Rail Photos

"GOLD COAST" IS RENAMED

Another situation presented itself in 1958, when the Gold Coast became independent and the new name of Ghana was chosen. *On the left*, we see Ghana's High Commissioner, Mr. E. O. Asafu-Adjaye doing the honours at Euston Station on December 12th, 1958. The new nameplate fitted to No.45610 was given a red background, whereas it was the practice during the early 'Jubilee' days to use black.

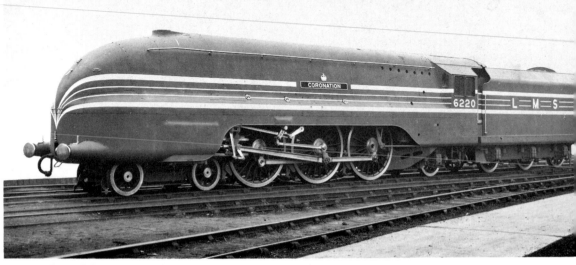

Above: First of the class, in striking blue and silver livery to match the coaches.

'CORONATION' CLASS

1937 was an important year for the L.M.S. It heralded the new 'Coronation Scot', which was hauled by a larger, streamlined version of the previous Pacifics.

Right: L.M.S. No.6230 (later B.R. No.46230), DUCHESS OF BUCCLEUCH was the first of five to be built without the streamlining in 1938.

Below: From 1944 to 1948, further batches were constructed as non-streamliners. They had some modifications and smoke deflectors. At the same time, all the original streamliners were rebuilt in a similar fashion.

British Rail Photos

Above: One of the streamlined 'Duchesses'. A total of 24 of the class were originally streamlined, but some of those built during the war, appeared in the black livery.

L. Hanson

Above: The only locomotive in the class to be re-named. L.M.S. No.6244 received its new nameplates in 1941.

Below: L.M.S. No.6243 was the last to remain streamlined. For eight months, it was the sole survivor, losing its streamlining in June, 1949.

British Rail Photos

46220 CORONATION ♔	46240 CITY OF COVENTRY*
46221 QUEEN ELIZABETH	46241 CITY OF EDINBURGH
46222 QUEEN MARY	46242 CITY OF GLASGOW
46223 PRINCESS ALICE	46243 CITY OF LANCASTER
46224 PRINCESS ALEXANDRA	46244 CITY OF LEEDS/
46225 DUCHESS OF GLOUCESTER	KING GEORGE VI
46226 DUCHESS OF NORFOLK	46245 CITY OF LONDON
46227 DUCHESS OF DEVONSHIRE	46246 CITY OF MANCHESTER
46228 DUCHESS OF RUTLAND	46247 CITY OF LIVERPOOL
46229 DUCHESS OF HAMILTON	46248 CITY OF LEEDS
46230 DUCHESS OF BUCCLEUCH	46249 CITY OF SHEFFIELD
46231 DUCHESS OF ATHOLL	46250 CITY OF LICHFIELD
46232 DUCHESS OF MONTROSE	46251 CITY OF NOTTINGHAM
46233 DUCHESS OF SUTHERLAND	46252 CITY OF LEICESTER
46234 DUCHESS OF ABERCORN	46253 CITY OF Sᵗ ALBANS
46235 CITY OF BIRMINGHAM*	46254 CITY OF STOKE-ON-TRENT*
46236 CITY OF BRADFORD	46255 CITY OF HEREFORD
46237 CITY OF BRISTOL	46256 SIR WILLIAM A.
46238 CITY OF CARLISLE	STANIER, F.R.S.
46239 CITY OF CHESTER	46257 CITY OF SALFORD

♔ *This locomotive carried a crown above the nameplate.*

* *These locomotives later carried a coat of arms above their nameplates.*

Right: L.M.S. No.6246 was also built in 1943 and painted black. Because it hampered maintenance, it was decided to remove the streamlining three years later.

British Rail Photos unless stated

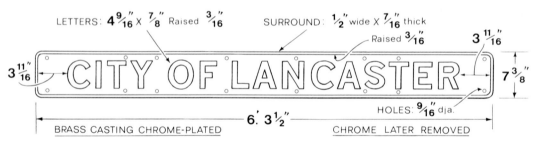

LETTERS: $4\frac{9}{16}''$ X $\frac{7}{8}''$ Raised $\frac{3}{16}''$ SURROUND: $\frac{1}{2}''$ wide X $\frac{7}{16}''$ thick

Raised $\frac{3}{16}''$ $3\frac{11}{16}''$

$3\frac{11}{16}''$ $7\frac{3}{8}''$

HOLES: $\frac{9}{16}''$ dia.

$6'\ 3\frac{1}{2}''$

BRASS CASTING CHROME-PLATED   CHROME LATER REMOVED

Notes: The thickness of the nameplates fitted to the original non-streamliners was $\frac{7}{8}$ in. instead of $\frac{7}{16}$ in. as above. The first twenty-five locomotives of the class had brass nameplates, chromium-plated, but this was polished away during the war although traces of chrome were left on the surrounds. The first five had dark blue backgrounds; the rest having black. When the locomotives were painted black during the war, red was used. After 1946, some were given maroon backgrounds.

Below: L.M.S. No.6240. One of three 'Cities' to receive a coat of arms.

No.46253 showing the small 'I'. *British Rail*

The matched pictures, *above and right* allow one to compare the streamlined with the non-streamlined. On the latter, the nameplates were slightly higher. *British Rail*

An unusual picture showing No.46251 standing in Nottingham Victoria Station. *T. Boustead*

Left: No.46235 again, as rebuilt, and with the coat of arms. *D. Eatwell*

Below: It was not until about a year after being built that No.46254 received the coat of arms. *British Rail*

The first of the class to be built, photographed after being de-streamlined in 1946, when a backplate was provided for the crown.   *R.O. Coffin*

No.46222 also taken after having the streamlining removed. Some of these early plates were of standard length and spaces were left where there was a short name *as above*.   *J. Oatway*

No.46224. First to be fitted with longer plates. This one was 7ft. $3\frac{3}{8}$ in. long. A large number of bolts were used to fix them. The above had 23!   *J. Oatway*

Finally, No.46256 one of the last two to be built. The nameplates were the longest in the class, 7ft. $5\frac{3}{8}$ in. long.

British Rail

THE EARLY YEARS

As with the other companies formed on January 1st, 1923, the L.N.E.R. also absorbed a number of railways which had hitherto named their locomotives. These two pages show some of the styles used.

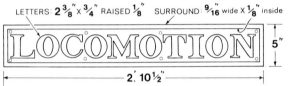

LETTERS: $2\frac{3}{8}$" x $\frac{3}{4}$" RAISED $\frac{1}{8}$"   SURROUND: $\frac{9}{16}$" wide x $\frac{1}{8}$" inside

5"

2' $10\frac{1}{2}$"

Above: The nameplate as originally fitted. Later, **1.** and **1825.** were added above and below the nameplate, respectively.

Only two locomotives of the Great Eastern Railway carried names. *Above:* PETROLEA, built in 1890, was named three years later when converted to an oil-burner.   *British Rail*

The other G.E.R. engine to receive a name was No.1900 built in 1900. The brass G.E.R. crest was removed in L.N.E.R. days, and new nameplates were fitted when the locomotive was rebuilt in 1933 (see Page 127).   *Real Photos*

LOCOMOTION, one of the famous pioneer engines. It was bu in 1825 by Robert Stephenson & Company for the Stockt & Darlington Railway, later amalgamated with the North Easte Railway.   *British R*

In 1845 DERWENT was added to the S. & D.R. stock. This had similar nameplates to LOCOMOTION being fitted to the sides of the wood lagging.   *G. Kitching*

In 1898, the Great Northern Railway introduced HENRY OAKLEY, a named Atlantic type locomotive. The idea of dividing the name between two splashers was not new, for the L. & N.W.R. had earlier built similar named locomotives. The nameplates had recessed letters filled with black wax.   *D. Eatwell*

After being rebuilt many times over the years, the North Eastern Railway finally settled for the above shaped nameplates in 1907.   *D. Eatwell*

In the early 1900's the Great Central Railway named some of their locomotives. *Above:* GLENALMOND, built in 1913, had nameplates with shaped ends, and these were fitted to the top of the straight splashers. *British Rail Photos*

The North British Railway's policy was to paint or transfer names on the splashers. The above belonged to the D30 'Scott' class built 1912-1920.

Another of the G.C.R.'s curved nameplates fitted in 1913. With most of them the splasher beading also formed part of the nameplate.
F.B.

From 1920, the Great North of Scotland Railway fitted nameplates to eight of their engines. These were neatly cast in brass and painted with a green background. The locomotives formed part of the L.N.E.R. 'D40' class. *F.B.*

Another G.C.R. nameplate, this time curved, fitted in 1906. It carried the company crest below, which was removed later by the L.N.E.R. when the nameplates were refixed on the face of the splashers.

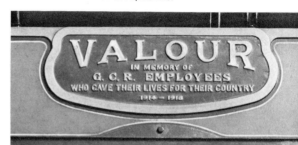

Built in 1920, the above was chosen as the Great Central Railway's war memorial locomotive. *L. Hanson*

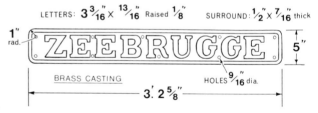

LETTERS: $3\frac{3}{16}$" × $\frac{13}{16}$" Raised $\frac{1}{8}$" SURROUND: $\frac{1}{2}$" × $\frac{7}{16}$" thick

1" rad. BRASS CASTING HOLES $\frac{9}{16}$" dia. 5" 3'. $2\frac{5}{8}$"

One of the Great Central 'Director' class.

Only a few months before the Big Four were formed in 1923, the Great Northern Railway decided to name two of their new Pacific type locomotives described on the next page. *British Rail*

The first of two built by the G.N.R. just before the Grouping. The other was No.1471 SIR FREDERICK BANBURY
British Rai

Original 'A1' and 'A3' CLASS

First introduced by the G.N.R. in 1922, this Pacific design was soon adopted by the L.N.E.R. who took over a year later. Under the guidance of Sir Nigel Gresley who designed them, further ones were built from 1924. Originally classified 'A1', they became 'A3's' when higher pressure boilers were fitted between 1927 and 1948. However, in 1945, when Thompson rebuilt the above locomotive as his new prototype 'A1', the original 'A1's' still awaiting new boilers were temporarily re-classified 'A10'.

No.2567 (finally B.R. No.60068) showing the shorter styled chimney and cab roof later fitted to the class.
Real Photos

Apart from the first two of the class named by the Great Northern Railway, the L.N.E.R. were slow to name the others added to the class. Eventually, all except five were named after famous racehorses; the plates being fitted to the centre wheel splasher *as above*.   *T. Boustead*

At first, the L.N.E.R. produced several sizes of nameplate, but the shorter ones, in particular, started to crack. In 1926, some were replaced with heavier, longer plates. MANNA *above*, shows how the short names were later spaced out.

HERMIT *above*, was one of the original short nameplates, and signs of the cracking can be seen below the letters. Without doubt, vibration had something to do with the trouble, for thicker top plates were also fitted to the splashers.

The first six photographs on this page are by R.F. Orpwood. Grateful thanks are extended to him and the Gresley Society for many of the pictures that follow.

No.60059

No.60097

No.60037 *above*, was one of a number which had the names displayed in the modern Gill Sans lettering. HYPERION was the famous racehorse that won both the Derby and St. Leger in 1933.

Below: The name of No.60048 could have been mistaken for the L.N.E.R. Works, but it was the racehorse that won the 1873 Derby!

Below: No.60040 was another of the nameplates to have Gill Sans letters.   *E. Lowden*

60035 WINDSOR LAD	60063 ISINGLASS	60090 GRAND PARADE
60036 COLOMBO	60064 WILLIAM WHITELAW/	60091 CAPTAIN CUTTLE
60037 HYPERION	TAGALIE	60092 FAIRWAY
60038 FIRDAUSSI	60065 KNIGHT OF THE THISTLE/	60093 CORONACH
60039 SANDWICH	KNIGHT OF THISTLE	60094 COLORADO
60040 CAMERONIAN	60066 MERRY HAMPTON	60095 FLAMINGO
60041 SALMON TROUT	60067 LADAS	60096 PAPYRUS
60042 SINGAPORE	60068 SIR VISTO	60097 HUMORIST
60043 BROWN JACK	60069 SCEPTRE	60098 SPION KOP
60044 MELTON	60070 GLADIATEUR	60099 CALL BOY
60045 LEMBERG	60071 TRANQUIL	60100 SPEARMINT
60046 DIAMOND JUBILEE	60072 SUNSTAR	60101 CICERO
60047 DONOVAN	60073 ST GATIEN	60102 SIR FREDERICK BANBURY †
60048 DONCASTER	60074 HARVESTER	60103 FLYING SCOTSMAN
60049 GALTEE MORE	60075 ST. FRUSQUIN	60104 SOLARIO
60050 PERSIMMON	60076 GALOPIN	60105 VICTOR WILD
60051 BLINK BONNY	60077 THE WHITE KNIGHT	60106 FLYING FOX
60052 PRINCE PALATINE	60078 NIGHT HAWK	60107 ROYAL LANCER
60053 SANSOVINO	60079 BAYARDO	60108 GAY CRUSADER
60054 MANNA/	60080 DICK TURPIN	60109 HERMIT
PRINCE OF WALES	60081 SHOTOVER	60110 ROBERT THE DEVIL
60055 WOOLWINDER	60082 NEIL GOW	60111 ENTERPRISE
60056 CENTENARY	60083 SIR HUGO	60112 ST SIMON
60057 ORMONDE	60084 TRIGO	4470 GREAT NORTHERN * †
60058 BLAIR ATHOL	60085 MANNA	
60059 TRACERY	60086 GAINSBOROUGH	
60060 THE TETRARCH	60087 BLENHEIM	
60061 PRETTY POLLY	60088 BOOK LAW	
60062 MINORU	60089 FELSTEAD	

*Original L.N.E.R. number. Rebuilt as new A1/1 class in September, 1945, and finally numbered: 60113.

†Named by the G.N.R.

Below: 'A3' class No.60066 MERRY HAMPTON on a Newcastle express near Potters Bar. It shows the refinements which most of the class received between 1958 and 1963.   *N.E. Preedy*

No.60112. One of the original short nameplates to survive. *C.L. Caddy*

No.60068. One of the longer and heavier replacements. *R.F. Orpwood*

No.60106. The first 'racehorse' name to be fitted, April, 1925. *E. Lowden*

No.60051. Two words in Gill Sans letters. *E. Lowden*

No.60052. Last of the class to survive in service. Withdrawn January, 1966. *R.F. Orpwood*

The above was carried by L.N.E.R. No.2563 before being renamed TAGALIE in July, 1941. A straight version of WILLIAM WHITELAW then appeared on an 'A4' class locomotive. *British Rail*

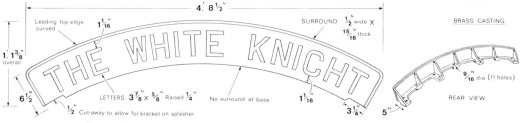

It was the general practice of the L.N.E.R. to paint the background of their nameplates black, but there were exceptions, when red was used.

Below: No.60054. One of five names not associated with racehorses; being renamed from MANNA in December 1926. MANNA again appeared on a new 'A3' locomotive built in February 1930. *T. Boustead*

Above: One of the original 'A2' class Pacifics, No.2402 **CITY OF YORK** as built by the L.N.E.R. in December, 1924.

British Rail

Original 'A2' CLASS

No.2404 **CITY OF RIPON** as fitted with a surplus Gresley 'A1' class boiler and other modifications in 1929.

Kelland Collection, Courtesy of Bournemouth Railway Club

Better known as the Raven Pacifics, after their designer, Sir Vincent Raven, the North Eastern Railway had built two of them just before the L.N.E.R. came into being in 1923. It was not until 1924, when a further three were constructed at Darlington, that all five received names. Unfortunately, despite a number of modifications, the locomotives were not a success. Development of the 'A1' class being preferred, they were all withdrawn by May, 1937.

2400 **CITY OF NEWCASTLE**
2401 **CITY OF KINGSTON UPON HULL**
2402 **CITY OF YORK**
2403 **CITY OF DURHAM**
2404 **CITY OF RIPON**

Above: The nameplates of the class were very distinctive being cast with rounded ends and moulded rim. *Photomatic*

Left: A unique way of displaying a long name!

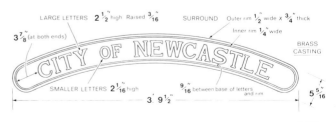

LARGE LETTERS 2½" high Raised 3/16   SURROUND Outer rim ½" wide x ¾" thick

Inner rim ¼" wide

3⅞"(at both ends)

BRASS CASTING

CITY OF NEWCASTLE

SMALLER LETTERS 2 1/16" high   9/16" between base of letters and rim

3' 9½"   5 5/16"

'D49' SHIRE CLASS

L.N.E.R. No.307 KINCARDINESHIRE in original livery. Finally B.R. No.62716
Real Photos

The first of this 4-4-0 class was completed at Darlington Works in October, 1927.
The nameplates depict most of the English and Scottish counties served by the L.N.E.R. with the exception of Berkshire. A number of modifications were made to the class over the years.

62700 YORKSHIRE
62701 DERBYSHIRE
62702 OXFORDSHIRE
62703 HERTFORDSHIRE
62704 STIRLINGSHIRE
62705 LANARKSHIRE
62706 FORFARSHIRE
62707 LANCASHIRE
62708 ARGYLLSHIRE
62709 BERWICKSHIRE
62710 LINCOLNSHIRE
62711 DUMBARTONSHIRE
62712 MORAYSHIRE
62713 ABERDEENSHIRE
62714 PERTHSHIRE
62715 ROXBURGHSHIRE
62716 KINCARDINESHIRE
62717 BANFFSHIRE
62718 KINROSS-SHIRE
62719 PEEBLES-SHIRE
62720 CAMBRIDGESHIRE
62721 WARWICKSHIRE
62722 HUNTINGDONSHIRE
62723 NOTTINGHAMSHIRE
62724 BEDFORDSHIRE
62725 INVERNESS-SHIRE
62726 LEICESTERSHIRE *
62727 BUCKINGHAMSHIRE *
62728 CHESHIRE
62729 RUTLANDSHIRE
62730 BERKSHIRE
62731 SELKIRKSHIRE
62732 DUMFRIES-SHIRE
62733 NORTHUMBERLAND
62734 CUMBERLAND
62735 WESTMORLAND

L.N.E.R. No.234, first of the class. Finally B.R. No.62700. *British Rail*

When the L.N.E.R. started displaying the locomotive number on the cabsides, the works plates were transferred to the splashers, below the nameplates.
Real Photos

*Renamed as 'Hunts'
(see opposite page)*

LETTERS:
3 7/8" high X
5/8" thick
Raised 3/16"

BRASS CASTING

HYPHEN 1" long

4' 9"

SURROUND:
1/2" wide and thick

HOLES:
1/2" dia.

6 7/16"

'D49' HUNT CLASS

From April 1932, further locomotives were constructed with rotary cam operated poppet valves. These 'D49's' could also be distinguished from the 'Shires' by their 'Hunt' nameplates.

No.62742 THE BRAES OF DERWENT, with the longest nameplate in the class. *Real Photos*

62726	THE	MEYNELL*
62727	THE	QUORN*
62736	THE	BRAMHAM MOOR
62737	THE	YORK AND AINSTY
62738	THE	ZETLAND
62739	THE	BADSWORTH
62740	THE	BEDALE
62741	THE	BLANKNEY
62742	THE	BRAES OF DERWENT
62743	THE	CLEVELAND
62744	THE	HOLDERNESS
62745	THE	HURWORTH
62746	THE	MIDDLETON
62747	THE	PERCY
62748	THE	SOUTHWOLD
62749	THE	COTTESMORE
62750	THE	PYTCHLEY
62751	THE	ALBRIGHTON
62752	THE	ATHERSTONE
62753	THE	BELVOIR
62754	THE	BERKELEY
62755	THE	BILSDALE
62756	THE	BROCKLESBY
62757	THE	BURTON
62758	THE	CATTISTOCK
62759	THE	CRAVEN
62760	THE	COTSWOLD
62761	THE	DERWENT
62762	THE	FERNIE
62763	THE	FITZWILLIAM
62764	THE	GARTH
62765	THE	GOATHLAND
62766	THE	GRAFTON
62767	THE	GROVE
62768	THE	MORPETH
62769	THE	OAKLEY
62770	THE	PUCKERIDGE
62771	THE	RUFFORD
62772	THE	SINNINGTON
62773	THE	SOUTH DURHAM
62774	THE	STAINTONDALE
62775	THE	TYNEDALE

Renamed from 'Shires'

Left-hand side of L.N.E.R. No.211 (finally B.R. No.62737). The cast brass fox faced forward on each side. *Real Photos*

No.62760, right-hand side. When the L.N.E.R. locomotives were re-numbered, sometimes an additional plate was fitted over the old number. Others had new works plates cast. *R. Panting*

SMALL LETTERS: $1\frac{15}{16}$" X $\frac{5}{16}$" Raised $\frac{3}{16}$"

LARGE LETTERS: $3\frac{7}{8}$" X $\frac{9}{16}$" Raised $\frac{3}{16}$"

Overall height 1'.4"

SURROUND: $\frac{1}{2}$" wide X $\frac{7}{16}$" thick   Raised $\frac{3}{16}$"   3' 0$\frac{1}{2}$"

HOLLOW-CAST BRASS FOX: 1'. 7$\frac{1}{2}$" long X 4$\frac{3}{4}$" overall $1\frac{1}{4}$" thick at widest point. Fixed with 2 bolts.

SOLID BRASS CASTING

6$\frac{1}{2}$"

HOLES: $\frac{1}{2}$" dia.

121

An original 'B17' class locomotive shortly after being renamed in 1938. *British Rail*

No.61648 ARSENAL showing the Westinghouse pump fitted to the right-hand side.
Photomatic

'B17' & 'B2' CLASSES

December 1928, saw a new 4-6-0 three cylinder type for express working in the Eastern Counties. The first names chosen were those of stately homes and mansions, but later, regiments and football clubs were also included.

A number of modifications were made to the locomotives over the years; the biggest being the introduction of new boilers, and some with only two cylinders which were re-classified 'B2'.

Below: In B.R. livery No.61657 DONCASTER ROVERS as built with larger straight-sided tender, and later rebuilt with 100A ('B1' type) boiler. *British Rail*

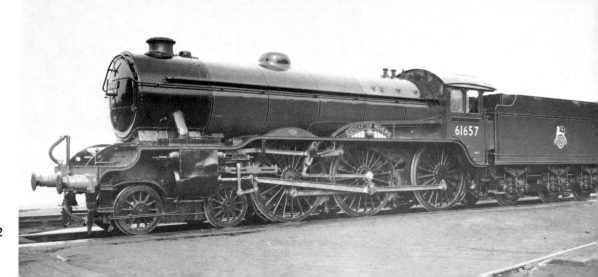

L.N.E.R. No.2802 (finally B.R. No.61602)   *E. Lowden*

L.N.E.R. No.1636 (later B.R. No.61636) the only 'Manor' in the class.

L.N.E.R. No.2800 (finally B.R. No.61600) was the first to be built, and was named after royal permission had been granted. *British Rail*

61600 SANDRINGHAM	61628 HAREWOOD HOUSE	61654 SUNDERLAND ○
61601 HOLKHAM	61629 NAWORTH CASTLE	61655 MIDDLESBROUGH ○
61602 WALSINGHAM	61630 THORESBY PARK/	61656 LEEDS UNITED ○
>61603 FRAMLINGHAM	TOTTENHAM HOTSPUR ○	61657 DONCASTER ROVERS ○
61604 ELVEDEN	61631 SERLBY HALL	61658 NEWCASTLE UNITED ○/
61605 BURNHAM THORPE/	>61632 BELVOIR CASTLE/	THE ESSEX REGIMENT*
LINCOLNSHIRE REGIMENT *	ROYAL SOVEREIGN	61659 NORWICH CITY ○/
61606 AUDLEY END	61633 KIMBOLTON CASTLE	EAST ANGLIAN
>61607 BLICKLING	61634 HINCHINGBROOKE	61660 HULL CITY ○
61608 GUNTON	61635 MILTON	61661 SHEFFIELD WEDNESDAY ○
61609 QUIDENHAM	61636 HARLAXTON MANOR	61662 MANCHESTER UNITED ○
61610 HONINGHAM HALL	61637 THORPE HALL	61663 EVERTON ○
61611 RAYNHAM HALL	61638 MELTON HALL	61664 LIVERPOOL ○
61612 HOUGHTON HALL	>61639 RENDELSHAM HALL/	61665 LEICESTER CITY ○
61613 WOODBASTWICK HALL	NORWICH CITY ○	61666 NOTTINGHAM FOREST ○
>61614 CASTLE HEDINGHAM	61640 SOMERLEYTON HALL	61667 BRADFORD ○
>61615 CULFORD HALL	61641 GAYTON HALL	61668 BRADFORD CITY ○
>61616 FALLODON	61642 KILVERSTONE HALL	61669 BARNSLEY ○
>61617 FORD CASTLE	61643 CHAMPION LODGE	61670 MANCHESTER CITY ○/
61618 WYNYARD PARK	>61644 EARLHAM HALL	TOTTENHAM HOTSPUR ○/
61619 WELBECK ABBEY	61645 THE SUFFOLK REGIMENT *	CITY OF LONDON
61620 CLUMBER	61646 GILWELL PARK	>61671 MANCHESTER CITY ○/
61621 HATFIELD HOUSE	61647 HELMINGHAM HALL	ROYAL SOVEREIGN
61622 ALNWICK CASTLE	61648 ARSENAL ○	61672 WEST HAM UNITED ○
61623 LAMBTON CASTLE	61649 SHEFFIELD UNITED ○	
61624 LUMLEY CASTLE	61650 GRIMSBY TOWN ○	○*These locomotives carried a brass*
61625 RABY CASTLE	61651 DERBY COUNTY ○	*replica football below the nameplate.*
61626 BRANCEPETH CASTLE	61652 DARLINGTON ○	
61627 ASKE HALL	61653 HUDDERSFIELD TOWN ○	**These displayed a regimental crest*
		beneath the nameplate.

> Rebuilt and Classified 'B2'

A FOOTBALL CLUB BECOMES A REGIMENT

Only a few L.N.E.R. locomotives carried military names, and three of them were included in the 'B17' class. The two illustrated here replaced existing names.

Above: The scene is Romford Station, during an exhibition of rolling stock on June 6/7th, 1936, L.N.E.R. No.2858 having carried the football name NEWCASTLE UNITED for less than two weeks, was renamed THE ESSEX REGIMENT.

Right: A close-up of the nameplate and crest just after the unveiling.

Below: Previously named BURNHAM THORPE, L.N.E.R. No.2805 was officially renamed LINCOLNSHIRE REGIMENT at Lincoln Station on April 30th, 1938.

Above: Fox Photos   Below: British Rail

No.61652   *M.J. Robinson*

No.61653   *I.S. Carr*

No.61654   *I.S. Carr*

The above name first appeared in public during a rolling stock exhibition at Walthamstow on May 29th, 1937. Having only been built during that month, the locomotive, L.N.E.R. No.2870, first carried the name MANCHESTER CITY, but only for 16 days. Subsequently, this was one of two locomotives streamlined and renamed, details of which are on the next page.   *L. & G.R.P.*

There was a slight variation with the first 'B17' rebuilt as a 'B2' and named MANCHESTER CITY for a short while. Each of the nameplates had its own support, upon which the football and colours were displayed.

J.H. Gibbons

No.61662 *above*, was one of the few 'footballers' to have continuous beading at the base of the nameplate. Most of the others had the bottom corners cut away to allow for the splasher bracket. The length of MANCHESTER UNITED also differed: 4ft. 11⅛in. and the condensed style lettering measured 4in. high by ⅝in. thick.

The other pattern of football nameplates however, were of standard length *as shown on the left;* the letters for the shorter names being spaced out. The club colours were displayed on the splashers at each side of the cast brass replica football.

A ¾-view of L.N.E.R. No.2859. The nameplates were subsequently transferred to L.N.E.R. No.2839 (finally B.R. No.61639).   *British Rail*

No.61656   *F.B.*

'B17s' STREAMLINED

In September, 1937, two 'B17' class locomotive No's 2859 NORWICH CITY and 2870 TOTTENHAM HOTSPUR were chosen to haul the new 'East Anglian' train between London and Norwich. Both received streamlined casing and straight nameplates:

2859 EAST ANGLIAN   2870 CITY OF LONDON

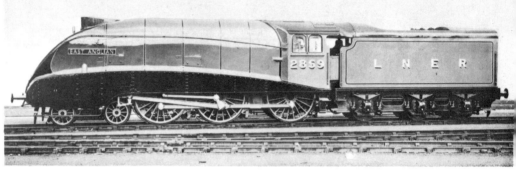

Above: No.2859 NORWICH CITY as built.

Right: The same locomotive, streamlined and renamed EAST ANGLIAN

British Rail Photos

During the first week of streamlining, both locomotives were tried out with straight versions of the football club nameplates, but these were replaced with more relevant names as above. *Photomatic*

When the streamlining was removed in 1951, curved nameplates were again fitted. The names were retained as the original 'footballers' had been refitted to others of the class in 1938. *J. Oatway*

FURTHER 'B17' REBUILDS

When Edward Thompson took over from Sir Nigel Gresley in 1945, he set about improving some of the 'B17's' with higher pressure boilers. One version was a two-cylinder rebuild, classified 'B2', which, with its straight framing also improved its appearance.

L.N.E.R. No.2871 MANCHESTER CITY was the first rebuilt in August 1945. Later, it became No.1671 ROYAL SOVEREIGN for hauling the Royal Train.

Above: In its final livery, No.61671 ROYAL SOVEREIGN *Photomatic*

Right: When the locomotive was taken out of service in 1958, the nameplates were transferred to another 'B2' class engine, No.61632. *G.O.P. Pearce*

'K2' CLASS

Although introduced by the G.N.R. in 1912, this class of 2-6-0 type locomotive did not carry names until 1933/34. Thirteen were named after Lochs near to the West Highland Line where the L.N.E.R. had transferred them.

61764	LOCH ARKAIG	61787	LOCH QUOICH
61772	LOCH LOCHY	61788	LOCH RANNOCH
61774	LOCH GARRY	61789	LOCH LAIDON
61775	LOCH TREIG	61790	LOCH LOMOND
61781	LOCH MORAR	61791	LOCH LAGGAN
61782	LOCH EIL	61794	LOCH OICH
61783	LOCH SHEIL		

Above: L.N.E.R. No.4691 (finally B.R. No.61781) LOCH MORAR as named in 1933.
Photomatic

Right: Close-up of the nameplate fitted to No.61788.
D. Capper

LETTERS: $3\frac{15}{16}$" high X
$\frac{5}{8}$" thick
Raised $\frac{1}{4}$"

SURROUND: $\frac{3}{8}$" wide X
$\frac{9}{16}$" thick
Curved edges

BRASS CASTING

HOLES: $\frac{1}{2}$" dia.

Raised $\frac{1}{4}$" inside

$6\frac{1}{2}$"

$4' 8\frac{1}{8}$"

'D16' CLASS

One locomotive of the 'D16' class was named, and although this was a rebuild of an earlier G.E.R. design, it is included here as the L.N.E.R. replaced the older style nameplates (see page 112) with their own heavier cast pattern.

62546 CLAUD HAMILTON

Above: L.N.E.R. No.8900 CLAUD HAMILTON as rebuilt in 1933.
Ian Allan Library

Right: When the above locomotive was scrapped in 1947, the nameplates were transferred to No.2546 of the same class.
Photomatic

'P2' CLASS

These 2-8-2 type locomotives first made their appearance in 1934. Designed by Gresley for the difficult line north of Edinburgh, it was the first time the L.N.E.R. had used straight nameplates, displaying the new Gill Sans lettering.

2001 COCK O' THE NORTH
2002 EARL MARISCHAL
2003 LORD PRESIDENT
2004 MONS MEG
2005 THANE OF FIFE
2006 WOLF OF BADENOCH

Above: L.N.E.R. No.2001 **COCK O' THE NORTH** as built with its unique front, which it was hoped would deflect the smoke.

It was not until two years after the first pair of locomotives that another one was built. This was L.N.E.R. No.2003 LORD PRESIDENT *seen on the right* which had a re-designed front end, based on the success of the 'A4s'. *Above:* Last of the class to be built in September 1936, No.2006 WOLF OF BADENOCH shows the final shape of these locomotives before they were rebuilt as the 'A2/2' class.

British Rail Photos

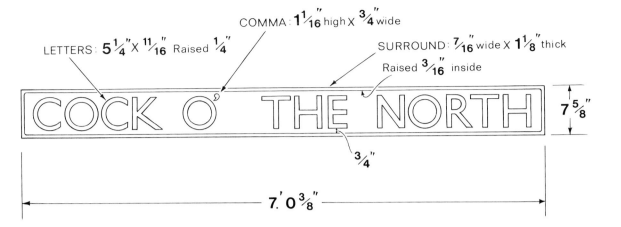

LETTERS: $5\frac{1}{4}$" X $\frac{11}{16}$" Raised $\frac{1}{4}$"

COMMA: $1\frac{1}{16}$" high X $\frac{3}{4}$" wide

SURROUND: $\frac{7}{16}$" wide X $1\frac{1}{8}$" thick

Raised $\frac{3}{16}$" inside

COCK O' THE NORTH

$7\frac{5}{8}$"

$\frac{3}{4}$"

$7' 0\frac{3}{8}$"

Left: Rebuilt No.60503 **LORD PRESIDENT** in its final form.

Below: The name-plates, with an extra curved backing piece, were fitted to the sides of the smokebox.
Photos: T. Boustead

Rebuilt as 'A2/2' CLASS

Although the 'A2' class is dealt with on pages 142–3, the 'A2/2' group are reviewed here as the locomotives were a direct rebuild of the 'P2' class. Edward Thompson reconstructed them as 4-6-2 engines in 1943–44. Very little remained of the original front end design. In fact, the first two dealt with No's 2005 and 2006, did not carry their names again until June 1944, but the other four rebuilt that year, appeared with their name-plates.

Above: First of the class, L.N.E.R. 2509 (finally B.R. No.60014) SILVER LINK in special silver-grey finish to match the coaches of the new 'Silver Jubilee' express.
British Rail

'A4' CLASS

QUICKSILVER

Above: Another of the first four to go into service with the name painted on the sides.
Photomatic

The first appearance of L.N.E.R. No.2509 SILVER LINK outside the Doncaster Works in September, 1935. Note the nameplate, which was later replaced, for two years by hand-painted letters on the sides.

British Rail

Right: L.N.E.R. No.29 (later B.R. No.60029) WOODCOCK in Garter Blue livery and with wheel valances removed. A close-up of the nameplate appears on the page opposite.

M.W. Earley

SILVER LINK

No other locomotive caused such a sensation as **SILVER LINK** when it first appeared in September, 1935. During its demonstration run with the 'Silver Jubilee' stock on September 27th, it averaged over 100 m.p.h. for 41 miles, and twice attained 112½ m.p.h. For the first few days of its life, chromium-plated nameplates were fitted, but for some reason these were replaced with painted letters on the sides. In 1937 however, a further set of brass nameplates of the same pattern was fitted. **SILVER LINK** and **QUICKSILVER** were the only two of the class to have nameplates with rounded corners.

Between 1939 and 1948, thirteen of the 'A4' class were renamed mostly after Directors of the L.N.E.R. As a result, when the class was renumbered, the majority of the 'new' names were placed at the top of the list, *as below*. It should also be noted that the B.R. numbers listed were only carried by the final names, since the original ones had L.N.E.R. numbers only.

60001 GARGANEY/SIR RONALD MATTHEWS	60018 SPARROW HAWK
60002 POCHARD/SIR MURROUGH WILSON	60019 BITTERN
60003 OSPREY/ANDREW K. McCOSH	60020 GUILLEMOT
60004 GREAT SNIPE/WILLIAM WHITELAW	60021 WILD SWAN
60005 CAPERCAILLIE/CHARLES H. NEWTON/	60022 MALLARD★
SIR CHARLES NEWTON	60023 GOLDEN EAGLE
60006 HERRING GULL/SIR RALPH WEDGWOOD	60024 KINGFISHER★
60007 SIR NIGEL GRESLEY	60025 FALCON
60008 GOLDEN SHUTTLE/DWIGHT D. EISENHOWER	60026 KESTREL/MILES BEEVOR
60009 UNION OF SOUTH AFRICA★	60027 MERLIN★
60010 WOODCOCK/DOMINION OF CANADA★	60028 SEA EAGLE/WALTER K. WHIGHAM
60011 EMPIRE OF INDIA★	60029 WOODCOCK
60012 COMMONWEALTH OF AUSTRALIA★	60030 GREAT SNIPE/GOLDEN FLEECE
60013 DOMINION OF NEW ZEALAND★	60031 GOLDEN PLOVER
60014 SILVER LINK	60032 GANNET
60015 QUICKSILVER	60033 SEAGULL
60016 SILVER KING	60034 PEREGRINE/LORD FARINGDON
60017 SILVER FOX★	4469 GADWALL/SIR RALPH WEDGWOOD†

★ *At some time during their service these locomotives carried an additional plaque, motif, or coat of arms.*

†*L.N.E.R. No.4469 was bombed at York on April 29th, 1942. It was scrapped shortly afterwards, and the name transferred to No.4466 (finally B.R. No.60006).*

No.60021

No.60029

No.60025

No.60033

Photos: R.F. Orpwood

NEW PLATES FOR OLD!

L.N.E.R. No.4496 (finally B.R. No.60008) was renamed as above in September, 1945. *R.F. Orpwood*

Above: L.N.E.R. No.4498 (finally B.R. No.60007) as it first appeared with solid brass nameplates. In January, 1939, these were replaced with base plates upon which stainless steel letters and beading were screwed *as below.* Photomatic

L.N.E.R. No.4494 (finally B.R. No.60003) was renamed as above in October, 1942. *R.F. Orpwood*

L.N.E.R. No.26 (later B.R. No.60026) was renamed as above in November, 1947. *R.F. Orpwood*

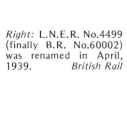

Above: A close-up section of the new nameplates. The screws can clearly be seen. *N.E. Preedy*

Right: L.N.E.R. No.4499 (finally B.R. No.60002) was renamed in April, 1939. *British Rail*

132

Above: No.60013 with one of the long names cast by B.R. in October 1952, replacing the original nameplates that were produced in two sections.

R.F. Orpwood

Right: L.N.E.R. No.4490 (finally B.R. No.60011) was officially named EMPIRE OF INDIA at Kings Cross Station on June 28th, 1937 by Sir Firoz Khan Noon, High Commissioner for India. The nameplates, as with some of the others in the class, were chromium-plated.

British Rail

Apart from the 'silver', 'bird' and 'personality' names, another group was named after Commonwealth countries. In addition to their nameplates, these carried coats of arms on the cabsides *as shown on the next page.*

No.60009, *above,* was another to have two-piece nameplates. In April, 1954, the locomotive received a metal plaque fitted to the left-hand side.
Nameplate photo: G.O.P. Pearce   *Plaque: R.F. Orpwood*

Below: No.60012 with the longest nameplate fitted. It measured 10ft. 2¾in. overall; being in two sections: 5ft. 5½in. and 4ft. 9¼in.   *R.F. Orpwood*

⌐JOINED HERE

133

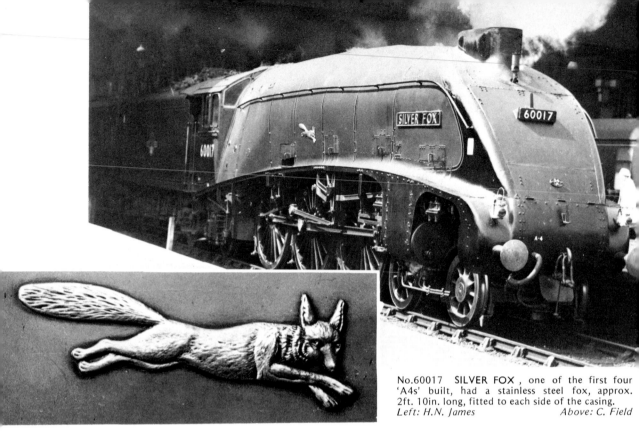

No.60017 **SILVER FOX** , one of the first four 'A4s' built, had a stainless steel fox, approx. 2ft. 10in. long, fitted to each side of the casing.
Left: H.N. James   *Above: C. Field*

FURTHER 'A4' CLASS EMBELLISHMENTS

Above: L.N.E.R. No.4489 (finally B.R. No.60010) carried a bell presented by the Canadian Pacific Railway Co. in March, 1938. At the same time, the brass nameplates were replaced by ones with stainless steel letters and beading screwed onto base plates.

Stainless steel figures were fitted to the cabsides and also hand-painted panels of the Canadian coat of arms.
Others are shown below   *Photos by H.N. James*

No.60009
R.F. Orpwood

No.60011
Photomatic

No.60012
J. Davenport

No.60013
Photomatic

HIGH SPEED STEAM

The achievement of L.N.E.R. No.4468 (finally B.R. No.60022) goes without saying. The plaque *on the right*, fitted in March, 1948, was fixed in the central position on the streamlined casing.

Above: E. Lowden   *Top right: F.B.*

The background colour of the 'A4' nameplates was black, but this was changed to light red for those locomotives working the special trains. When repainted in B.R. livery, however, black was used once more.

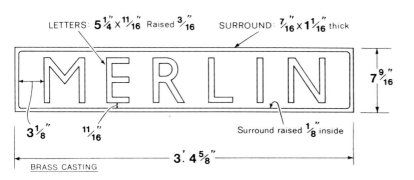

LETTERS: $5\frac{1}{4}'' \times 11\frac{1}{16}''$ Raised $\frac{3}{16}''$ SURROUND: $\frac{7}{16}'' \times 1\frac{1}{16}''$ thick

$7\frac{9}{16}''$

$3\frac{1}{8}''$ $\frac{11}{16}''$ Surround raised $\frac{1}{8}''$ inside

$3'\ 4\frac{5}{8}''$

BRASS CASTING

L.N.E.R. No.27 (later B.R. No.60027) **MERLIN** showing its badge as first displayed below the number.   *British Rail*

The above badge was fitted to the cabsides in May, 1946, but in June, 1948, was transferred to the sides of the boiler casing.   *F.B.*

In October, 1954, No.60024 *above,* also had plaques fitted to both sides of the casing.   *C.L. Caddy*

Right:
B. Hilton

'V2' CLASS

The first of this 2-6-2 type class appeared in 1936, but when it came to allocating names, the 'V2s', like the L.M.S. 'Black 5s', almost missed out! Undoubtedly, the large number of locomotives involved, together with the absence of wheel splashers (so convenient for attaching nameplates) were the main reasons. Only seven of this class were named between 1936 and 1939, and one other in 1958.

Above: The first locomotive of the class and the only one to have its nameplates displayed on the smokebox. *F.B.*

Above: L.N.E.R. No.4780 (finally B.R. No.60809). Officially named at Paragon Station, Hull on September 11th, 1937.
Photomatic

Below: The nameplates of this locomotive and also No.60835 were each cast in three sections and bolted to a steel backplate which was painted in the regimental colours. Overall measurements: 3ft. 11¼in. wide by 1ft. 11in. high. *Real Photos*

60800 GREEN ARROW

60809 THE SNAPPER
THE EAST YORKSHIRE REGIMENT
THE DUKE OF YORK'S OWN

60835 THE GREEN HOWARD
ALEXANDRA, PRINCESS OF WALES'S
OWN YORKSHIRE REGIMENT

60847 ST PETER'S SCHOOL
YORK A.D. 627

60860 DURHAM SCHOOL

60872 KING'S OWN YORKSHIRE
LIGHT INFANTRY

60873 COLDSTREAMER

60964 THE DURHAM LIGHT INFANTRY

Note: All the above locomotives, except No.60800, carried a crest or badge.

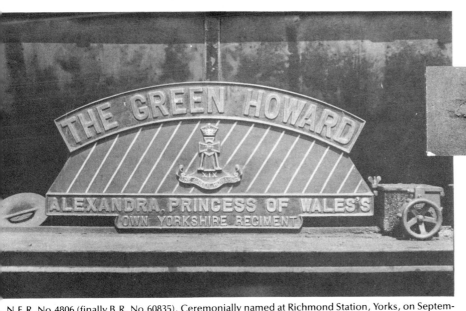

Above: No.60835 was one of two in the class to have small commemorative plates fitted to the cabsides.
B. Hilton

..N.E.R. No.4806 (finally B.R. No.60835). Ceremonially named at Richmond Station, Yorks, on Septem-er 24th, 1938.
M.J. Robertson

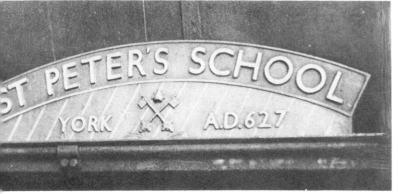

Above: L.N.E.R. No.4818 (finally B.R. No.60847). Officially named at York Station on April 3rd, 1939.
C. Field

Right: The naming ceremony of L.N.E.R. No.4831 (finally B.R. No.60860) DURHAM SCHOOL was held at Elvet Station, Durham on June 15th, 1939.

Below: L.N.E.R. No.4843 (finally B.R. No.60872). The unveiling of the name-plates took place in the Doncaster Works Yard on May 20th, 1939.
E. Neve

Above: Three nameplates of the 'V2' class which were exhibited at the old York Museum after the locomotives had been withdrawn.
These were cast in solid brass including the base, upon which the crests and colours were displayed.
D. Eatwell

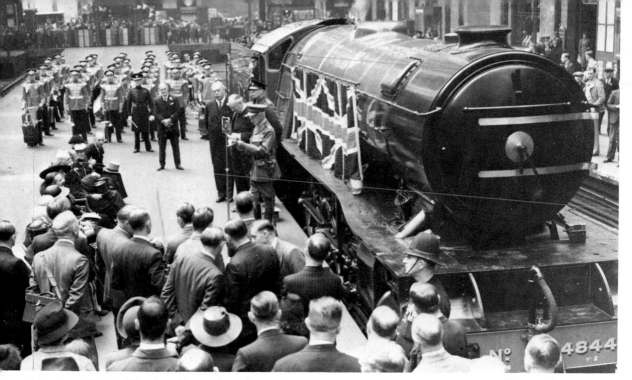

Major-General Sir Cecil Pereira, addresses the audience prior to unveiling the nameplate.

Keystone Press Photo

'V2' CLASS CHRISTENINGS

Seven of the 'V2' locomotives were ceremonially named after schools and regiments. Kings Cross Station was the venue for naming L.N.E.R. No.4844 COLDSTREAMER, *above*, on June 20th, 1939.

'V2' class No.60964, however, was named during the days of British Railways. Durham Station was chosen for the christening of THE DURHAM LIGHT INFANTRY on April 29th, 1958. The locomotive also had small cabside plates which read:

> THIS ENGINE WAS NAMED
> THE DURHAM LIGHT INFANTRY
> TO COMMEMORATE THE BI-CENTENARY
> OF THE RAISING OF THE REGIMENT
> 1758–1958

Col. K.M.W. Leather, with the Lord Mayor of Durham, admire the chromed nameplate soon after the unveiling.

K. Hoole

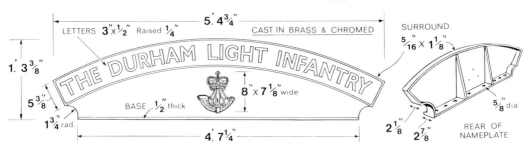

5.' 4¾"

LETTERS 3"x½" Raised ¼"   CAST IN BRASS & CHROMED

1.' 3⅜"

5⅜"

THE DURHAM LIGHT INFANTRY

8" x 7⅛" wide

BASE ½" thick

1¾" rad.

4.' 7¼"

SURROUND

5/16" X 1⅛"

5/8" dia

2⅛"   2⅞"

REAR OF NAMEPLATE

Built between 1937 and 1938, for the West Highland Line, the six 2-6-0 type locomotives of this class had straight nameplates fitted to the smokebox.
In 1945, one of the class was rebuilt with a new boiler and two cylinders. It was reclassified 'K1'.

Above: L.N.E.R. No.3441 (finally B.R. No.61993)
Rev. A.C. Cawston

'K4' & 'K1' CLASSES

L.N.E.R. No.3442 (finally B.R. No.61994) which is preserved.   *L.M. Hobdey*

61993 LOCH LONG	61996 LORD OF THE ISLES
61994 MacCAILEIN MÓR/	61997 MacCAILIN MÓR *
THE GREAT MARQUESS	61998 LORD OF DUNVEGAN/
61995 CAMERON OF LOCHIEL	MacLEOD OF MacLEOD

*Reclassified 'K1'

'V4' CLASS

There were only two locomotives in the 'V4' class, introduced in 1941, but only one of them was named. Like the above 'K4' class, they were used in Scotland where the combination of light axle loading and high tractive effort was required.

61700 BANTAM COCK

Above: L.N.E.R. No.3401 (finally B.R. No.61700) BANTAM COCK

Right: Close-up of the nameplate.
British Rail Photos

In L.N.E.R. apple green livery No.1032 (later B.R.61032) STEMBOK. *Photomatic*

'B1' CLASS

Designed by Edward Thompson, who succeeded Sir Nigel Gresley in 1941, there was a slow start to the building of these general purpose locomotives, on account of the war. By 1952 however, a total of 410 had been delivered by the L.N.E.R. works and private builders. A large proportion never received names. The first locomotives built had names of Antelope species, and late in 1947, eighteen more were given the names of L.N.E.R. directors.

61000 SPRINGBOK	61019 NILGHAI	61038 BLACKTAIL
61001 ELAND	61020 GEMSBOK	61039 STEINBOK
61002 IMPALA	61021 REITBOK	61040 ROEDEER
61003 GAZELLE	61022 SASSABY	61189 SIR WILLIAM GRAY
61004 ORYX	61023 HIROLA	61215 WILLIAM HENTON CARVER
61005 BONGO	61024 ADDAX	61221 SIR ALEXANDER ERSKINE-HILL
61006 BLACKBUCK	61025 PALLAH	61237 GEOFFREY H KITSON
61007 KLIPSPRINGER	61026 OUREBI	61238 LESLIE RUNCIMAN
61008 KUDU	61027 MADOQUA	61240 HARRY HINCHLIFFE
61009 HARTEBEESTE	61028 UMSEKE	61241 VISCOUNT RIDLEY
61010 WILDEBEESTE	61029 CHAMOIS	61242 ALEXANDER REITH GRAY
61011 WATERBUCK	61030 NYALA	61243 SIR HAROLD MITCHELL
61012 PUKU	61031 REEDBUCK	61244 STRANG STEEL
61013 TOPI	61032 STEMBOK	61245 MURRAY OF ELIBANK
61014 ORIBI	61033 DIBATAG	61246 LORD BALFOUR OF BURLEIGH
61015 DUIKER	61034 CHIRU	61247 LORD BURGHLEY
61016 INYALA	61035 PRONGHORN	61248 GEOFFREY GIBBS
61017 BUSHBUCK	61036 RALPH ASSHETON	61249 FITZHERBERT WRIGHT
61018 GNU	61037 JAIROU	61250 A. HAROLD BIBBY
		61251 OLIVER BURY
		61379 MAYFLOWER

END VIEW

LETTERS 4"x9⁄16" Raised 1⁄4". SURROUND 1⁄2" wide. SPACING 2 5⁄8" between letters

1 1⁄8"

GAZELLE

6 1⁄2"

1 1⁄2"   3 1⁄2"   3. 6 3⁄4"   3⁄4" between letters and surround

CAST IN BRASS

No.61018, shortest name to be fitted.
A.J. Bell-Wilson

No.61040. First of the 'B1s' to be built by the North British Locomotive Company, Glasgow. *B. Hilton*

No.61001 *Photomatic*

No.61189, one of the 'Director' names of the 'B1' class. *Photomatic*

The 'Director' nameplates were smaller. No.61238 *above* was 3ft. $8^7/_{16}$in. long by $5^1/_8$in. wide. The letters were only 3in. high. *E. Lowden*

Left: Press Association Photo

NAMING OF A 'B1'

On July 13th, 1951, No.61379 one of the 'B1' class which regularly served Boston was named **MAYFLOWER**.
It commemorated the association with the Pilgrim Fathers and the bond of goodwill linking the town of Boston, Lincs, and its namesake in Massachusetts, U.S.A. Commander Harold L. Goodwin, United States Navy, performed the ceremony at Kings Cross Station.

This small brass plate was also affixed to the side of the cab above the number. *B. Hilton*

'A2' class No.60527 SUN CHARIOT, built in 1948 to the designs of A.H. Peppercorn.   *R.O. Coffin*

'A2' CLASS

After the departure of the Raven Pacifics in 1937, the 'A2' classification was not used again until 1943, soon after Thompson had rebuilt Gresley's 'P2' class as 4-6-2s. In 1945, these were again reclassified 'A2/2'. Between 1944 and 1945, four locomotives intended to be 'V2s' were completed as Pacifics and classified 'A2/1'. Then, in May 1946, Thompson's own 'A2' design emerged, but in 1947, after his retirement, they were called 'A2/3' class locomotives. This made way for Peppercorn's new 4-6-2 design, which then became the final 'A2' class proper.

THOMPSON A2/1 CLASS

60507 HIGHLAND CHIEFTAIN
60508 DUKE OF ROTHESAY
60509 WAVERLEY
60510 ROBERT THE BRUCE

THOMPSON A2/2 CLASS
(REBUILT FROM GRESLEY P2 CLASS)

60501 COCK O' THE NORTH
60502 EARL MARISCHAL
60503 LORD PRESIDENT
60504 MONS MEG
60505 THANE OF FIFE
60506 WOLF OF BADENOCH

THOMPSON A2/3 CLASS

60500 EDWARD THOMPSON
60511 AIRBORNE
60512 STEADY AIM
60513 DANTE
60514 CHAMOSSAIRE
60515 SUN STREAM
60516 HYCILLA
60517 OCEAN SWELL
60518 TEHRAN
60519 HONEYWAY
60520 OWEN TUDOR
60521 WATLING STREET
60522 STRAIGHT DEAL
60523 SUN CASTLE
60524 HERRINGBONE

PEPPERCORN A2 CLASS

60525 A. H. PEPPERCORN
60526 SUGAR PALM
60527 SUN CHARIOT
60528 TUDOR MINSTREL
60529 PEARL DIVER
60530 SAYAJIRAO
60531 BAHRAM
60532 BLUE PETER
60533 HAPPY KNIGHT
60534 IRISH ELEGANCE
60535 HORNETS BEAUTY
60536 TRIMBUSH
60537 BACHELORS BUTTON
60538 VELOCITY
60539 BRONZINO

'A2' class No.60532 **BLUE PETER**, built in March, 1948, is now preserved in L.N.E.R. livery.   *T. Boustead*

The nameplates of the 'A2', 'A2/1' and 'A2/3' groups were fitted to the sides of the smoke deflectors *as above,* but as the rebuilt 'A2/2' locomotives had no side deflectors, their name-plates were fitted to the sides of the smokebox instead (see page 129). The above style of chimney was fitted to a number of the 'A2' class.

LETTERS: $5\frac{5}{16}$" x $\frac{11}{16}$" x $\frac{1}{4}$".   SURROUND: $\frac{1}{2}$" x $1\frac{1}{16}$" thick

$\frac{5}{8}$"

$7\frac{5}{8}$"

$3\frac{3}{4}$" $\frac{11}{16}$"   Surround raised $\frac{1}{8}$ inside   CAST IN BRASS

4'. $1\frac{15}{16}$"

Apart from minor variations in casting, these nameplates had the same specifications as those fitted to the streamlined 'A4' class.

Above: No.60508
British Rail

Left: No.60527
Photomatic

143

No.60158 **ABERDONIAN**, one of the Peppercorn 'A1' Pacifics introduced between 1948 and 1949.   *B. Hilton*

'A1' CLASS

There was much criticism when Edward Thompson selected the original 'A1' class No.4470 **GREAT NORTHERN** for rebuilding, for this was the very first of Gresley's Pacifics, and the result, in September 1945, caused much controversy. In 1947, it was reclassified 'A1/1' as A.H. Peppercorn, who succeeded Thompson, was about to build his own 'A1' version.

THOMPSON A1/1 CLASS
(REBUILT FROM GRESLEY A1 CLASS)

60113 GREAT NORTHERN*

PEPPERCORN A1 CLASS

60114 W. P. ALLEN
60115 MEG MERRILIES
60116 HAL O' THE WYND
60117 BOIS ROUSSEL
60118 ARCHIBALD STURROCK
60119 PATRICK STIRLING
60120 KITTIWAKE
60121 SILURIAN
60122 CURLEW
60123 H. A. IVATT
60124 KENILWORTH

60125 SCOTTISH UNION
60126 SIR VINCENT RAVEN
60127 WILSON WORSDELL
60128 BONGRACE
60129 GUY MANNERING
60130 KESTREL
60131 OSPREY
60132 MARMION
60133 POMMERN
60134 FOXHUNTER
60135 MADGE WILDFIRE
60136 ALCAZAR
60137 REDGAUNTLET
60138 BOSWELL
60139 SEA EAGLE
60140 BALMORAL
60141 ABBOTSFORD
60142 EDWARD FLETCHER
60143 SIR WALTER SCOTT

60144 KING'S COURIER
60145 SAINT MUNGO
60146 PEREGRINE
60147 NORTH EASTERN*
60148 ABOYEUR
60149 AMADIS
60150 WILLBROOK
60151 MIDLOTHIAN
60152 HOLYROOD
60153 FLAMBOYANT
60154 BON ACCORD
60155 BORDERER
60156 GREAT CENTRAL*
60157 GREAT EASTERN*
60158 ABERDONIAN
60159 BONNIE DUNDEE
60160 AULD REEKIE
60161 NORTH BRITISH*
60162 SAINT JOHNSTOUN

* *These locomotives carried the railways' crest incorporated in the nameplates. (see page 146)*

The final 'A1' class had straight nameplates fitted to the side of the smoke deflectors as with No.60140 *above*. Apart from the first Peppercorn Pacific built in 1948, the rest of the class did not receive names until 1950. By 1952, they all carried plates covering a wide, and well chosen, variety of names.

T. Boustead

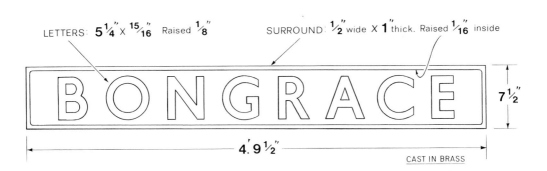

LETTERS: $5\frac{1}{4}$" x $^{15}/_{16}$" Raised $\frac{1}{8}$"   SURROUND: $\frac{1}{2}$" wide x 1" thick. Raised $^{1}/_{16}$" inside

BONGRACE

7$\frac{1}{2}$"

4' 9$\frac{1}{2}$"

CAST IN BRASS

No.60119   *E. Lowden*

No.60158   *E. Lowden*

'A1s' COMMEMORATE RAILWAYS OF THE PRE-GROUPING

Above: 'A1/1' class No.60113 after receiving smaller plates in August, 1950. These included the coat of arms of the G.N.R.
British Rail

These nameplates were cast in brass 1½in. thick. The discs fixed to these were of mild sheet steel.

Below: No.60161
J.L. Stephenson

Above: No.6014
N.E. Pre

Left: No.60156 clearly shows th disc upon which the coat of arm was displayed.
British Ra

Below: No.6015 This nameplate measured 4ft. 2i long by 1ft. 9in. deep with 4in. high letters.
E. Lowder

No.70028 ROYAL STAR, one of the Western Region 'Britannias' as originally built with handrails on the smoke deflectors. These were later removed for better visibility after the findings of the Milton, near Didcot, accident in 1955.
Photomatic

'BRITANNIA' CLASS 7P

When the 'Big Four' became British Railways in 1948, a decision was taken to standardise future locomotive design. Careful study of many types, together with locomotive exchanges, was carried out before the final choice. This first B.R. Pacific, turned out in 1951, was the result. It incorporated many good features, including an adaptation of Bulleid's successful boiler.

70000 BRITANNIA	70019 LIGHTNING	70038 ROBIN HOOD
70001 LORD HURCOMB	70020 MERCURY	70039 SIR CHRISTOPHER WREN
70002 GEOFFREY CHAUCER	70021 MORNING STAR	70040 CLIVE OF INDIA
70003 JOHN BUNYAN	70022 TORNADO	70041 SIR JOHN MOORE
70004 WILLIAM SHAKESPEARE	70023 VENUS	70042 LORD ROBERTS
70005 JOHN MILTON	70024 VULCAN	70043 LORD KITCHENER
70006 ROBERT BURNS	70025 WESTERN STAR	70044 EARL HAIG
70007 COEUR-DE-LION	70026 POLAR STAR	70045 LORD ROWALLAN
70008 BLACK PRINCE	70027 RISING STAR	70046 ANZAC
70009 ALFRED THE GREAT	70028 ROYAL STAR	70047 ★
70010 OWEN GLENDOWER	70029 SHOOTING STAR	70048 THE TERRITORIAL ARMY
70011 HOTSPUR	70030 WILLIAM WORDSWORTH	1908-1958
70012 JOHN OF GAUNT	70031 BYRON	
70013 OLIVER CROMWELL	70032 TENNYSON	70049 SOLWAY FIRTH
70014 IRON DUKE	70033 CHARLES DICKENS	70050 FIRTH OF CLYDE
70015 APOLLO	70034 THOMAS HARDY	70051 FIRTH OF FORTH
70016 ARIEL	70035 RUDYARD KIPLING	70052 FIRTH OF TAY
70017 ARROW	70036 BOADICEA	70053 MORAY FIRTH
70018 FLYING DUTCHMAN	70037 HEREWARD THE WAKE	70054 DORNOCH FIRTH

★*This locomotive did not carry a name*

LETTERS: 4" x 3/4" Raised 1/8" 2 3/4" SURROUND: 5/16" wide x 1 1/16" thick 3/4" dia. Raised 1/8"

2" ROYAL STAR 5 15/16"

3' 1 3/4" CAST IN BRASS

Although it was the practice of British Railways to give nameplates a black background, quite a few of these and other standard designs were painted red.

Above: No.70000, first of the class.   *R.O. Coffin*

Left: Putting the finishing touches to the moulding for No.70000 BRITANNIA.   *British Rail*

No other class had such an assortment of names. Nevertheless, they aroused much interest, for many of them had been used in the past on pre-grouping locomotives.

Above: No.70018   *B. Hilton*

Above: No.70038   *E. Lowden*

Left: No.70014 on 'Golden Arrow' duty.   *B. Fletcher*

Below: No.70051   *B. Hilton*

A DUKE NAMES A 'BRITANNIA'

To commemorate the Jubilee of the Territorial Army, 'Britannia' class Pacific No. 70048, which had hitherto run unnamed was christened by The Duke of Norfolk at Euston Station on July 23rd, 1958. The double-line nameplate, with its red background, was the only one made of aluminium; the rest of the class being cast in brass.

Left: Keystone Press Photo

No. 70048

J. Alsop

THE CHIEF SCOUT UNVEILS ANOTHER

The naming ceremony of 'Britannia' class No. 70045 had taken place a year earlier on July 16th, 1957 at Euston Station. *On the left* we see Chief Scout, Lord Rowallan doing the honours.

It is interesting to note that the method of naming most of the British Railways locomotives was similar to the practice adopted during the latter days of the L.N.E.R. where the nameplates were bolted to the smoke deflectors from the inside.

Left: Central Press Photo

No.73119 ELAINE passing Boscombe in October 1959.   *Kelland Collection by courtesy of Bournemouth Railway Club.*

STANDARD CLASS 5

This B.R. 4-6-0 type Class 5, built between 1951 and 1957, totalled 172 locomotives, yet, as with the L.M.S. Class 5 upon which they were based, few were named. Twenty of those working on the Southern Region received nameplates fitted to the sides of the running plate, and these perpetuated the names previously carried by some of the 'King Arthur' class, which these new locomotives replaced.

No.73081   *R.O. Coffin*

73080	MERLIN	73110	THE RED KNIGHT
73081	EXCALIBUR	73111	KING UTHER
73082	CAMELOT	73112	MORGAN LE FAY
73083	PENDRAGON	73113	LYONNESSE
73084	TINTAGEL	73114	ETARRE
73085	MELISANDE	73115	KING PELLINORE
73086	THE GREEN KNIGHT	73116	ISEULT
73087	LINETTE	73117	VIVIEN
73088	JOYOUS GARD	73118	KING LEODEGRANCE
73089	MAID OF ASTOLAT	73119	ELAINE

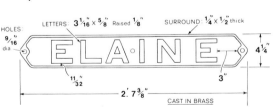

LETTERS: $3\frac{1}{16}$" × $\frac{5}{8}$" Raised $\frac{1}{8}$"   SURROUND: $\frac{1}{4}$" × $\frac{1}{2}$" thick

HOLES $\frac{9}{16}$" dia

$\frac{11}{32}$"

$4\frac{1}{4}$"

3"

2' $7\frac{3}{8}$"

CAST IN BRASS

Below: No.73110. Unlike the 'King Arthur' class, these new nameplates did not have the class panel below the name.   *C.L. Caddy*

No.72009 CLAN STEWART, last of the class to be built.

N.E. Preedy

'CLAN' CLASS 6P

Although designed to work over the many restricted routes, the 6P 'Clans' of British Railways, unlike the successful Bulleid 'Lightweight' Pacifics of the Southern Railway, never achieved any great distinction. In fact, an order for a further fifteen in 1955 was cancelled. Built at Crewe from December 1951, the ten locomotives were used north of the border, hence the choice of names.

72000 CLAN BUCHANAN	72005 CLAN MACGREGOR
72001 CLAN CAMERON	72006 CLAN MACKENZIE
72002 CLAN CAMPBELL	72007 CLAN MACKINTOSH
72003 CLAN FRASER	72008 CLAN MACLEOD
72004 CLAN MACDONALD	72009 CLAN STEWART

No.72008

B. Hilton

No.72006

E. Lowden

LETTERS: 4" x 3/4" Raised 1/8"   3 5/8"   SURROUND: 5/16" wide x 1 1/16" thick. Raised 1/8"

1 7/8"   CLAN MACGREGOR   5 15/16"

4' 9 1/2"   CAST IN BRASS

CLASS 8P

With the future of steam in doubt, it was surprising when in 1954 a new B.R. Class 8P 4-6-2 locomotive emerged from Crewe Works. This was an enlarged version of the earlier 'Britannia' class and fitted with Caprotti valve gear.

71000 DUKE OF GLOUCESTER

No.71000. The only one to be built. *British Rail*

Close-up of the nameplate. The middle 'E' was shorter than the others! *R.O. Coffin*

No.92220. The only one to be named. *British Rail*

CLASS 9F

One of the most popular of all British Railways designs was the Class 9F, also introduced in 1954. These 2-10-0 type locomotives were equally at home with passenger as well as heavy freight trains. Only the final one, built at Swindon Works in March 1960, was named.

92220 **EVENING STAR**

Below: Close-up showing the commemorative plaque fitted below the nameplate. Both were made of brass. *K.M. Buckle*

No.90732   *Photomatic*

AUSTERITY LOCOMOTIVES

During the war a large number of 2-8-0 and 2-10-0 type locomotives were built for the War Department, many of which became B.R. engines. Only three of the latter were named, two of them carrying the same name!

2-8-0 type	90732	VULCAN
2-10-0 type	90773	NORTH BRITISH
2-10-0 type	90774	NORTH BRITISH

No.90774   *H.C. Casserley*

The nameplates of VULCAN were carried on the cabsides *as above*, whereas those named NORTH BRITISH were fitted to the boiler sides.   *C. Field*

No. 9 **PRINCE OF WALES** , built in 1902, originally carried this name, but it was removed in 1913.   *C.L. Caddy*

'VALE OF RHEIDOL' CLASS

The locomotives of the Vale of Rheidol Narrow Gauge Railway ran for many years without names, and it was not until 1956 that they received their present nameplates, constructed in typical Great Western style.

7 OWAIN GLYNDŴR
8 LLYWELYN
9 PRINCE OF WALES

Above: No.7   *Right: No.8*   *Above: No.9*   *Photos by B. Hilton*

NAMED ELECTRIC AND DIESEL LOCOMOTIVES

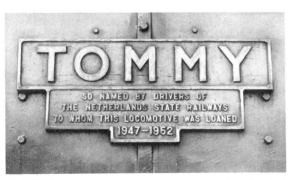

No.26000   *D.L. Percival*

No.26053   *Gregory, Wolverhampton*

CLASSES 76 & 77

No.26052. Cast in brass, this measures: 2ft. 3^3/$_8$in. long by 5^7/$_{16}$in. deep with 3^9/$_{16}$in. high letters.   *J. Oatway*

Running between Manchester and Sheffield, the first of Class 76 was built in 1941, whilst the remainder appeared 1950-53. Class 77 was introduced in 1953. 20 of the 65 locomotives were named *as below*.

26000 TOMMY	26052 **NESTOR**	27000 **ELECTRA**
26046 **ARCHIMEDES**	26053 **PERSEUS**	27001 **ARIADNE**
26047 **DIOMEDES**	26054 **PLUTO**	27002 **AURORA**
26048 **HECTOR**	26055 **PROMETHEUS**	27003 **DIANA**
26049 **JASON**	26056 **TRITON**	27004 **JUNO**
26050 **STENTOR**	26057 **ULYSSES**	27005 **MINERVA**
26051 **MENTOR**		27006 **PANDORA**

No's 27000-6 were sold to the Netherland Railways in 1969.

No. D219 (later No.40 019).   *Gregory, Wolverhampton*

CLASS 40

This class was introduced in 1958 for the London Midland Region, and only 25 of the 199 were named.

40 010 EMPRESS OF BRITAIN CPS	40 019 CARONIA CLS	40 028 SAMARIA CLS
40 011 MAURETANIA CL	40 020 FRANCONIA CLS	40 029 SAXONIA CLS
40 012 AUREOL EDL	40 021 IVERNIA CLS	40 030 SCYTHIA CLS
40 013 ANDANIA CLS	40 022 LACONIA CLS	40 031 SYLVANIA CLS
40 014 ANTONIA CLS	40 023 LANCASTRIA CLS	40 032 EMPRESS OF CANADA CPS
40 015 AQUITANIA CLS	40 024 LUCANIA CLS	40 033 EMPRESS OF ENGLAND CPS
40 016 CAMPANIA CLS	40 025 LUSITANIA CLS	40 034 ACCRA EDL
40 017 CARINTHIA CLS	40 027 PARTHIA CLS	40 035 APAPA EDL
40 018 CARMANIA CLS		

CPS = CANADIAN PACIFIC STEAMSHIPS   CL = CUNARD LINE   CLS = CUNARD LINES

EDL = ELDER DEMPSTER LINES

No.40 017. This measures: 2ft. 4¼in. long by 1ft. 2¾in. high overall with large letters 1^9/$_{16}$in. high. *D.L. Percival*

No.40 032. These plates were cast in aluminium with coloured house-flags.   *S. Dewey*

155

No. 812 at Radipole Halt, July 1972, on a Bristol-Weymouth stopping train. *C.L. Caddy*

No.D812, again, showing its double-line nameplate.
C.L. Caddy

No.D800 *D.H. Cape*

Below: D818 *C.L. Caddy*

'WARSHIP' CLASSES 42 & 43

Following the first five, introduced in 1958/9, a new batch known as Class 42 appeared. In 1960, a further 53, Classified 43, joined the rest on the Western Region.

D600	ACTIVE	D833	PANTHER
D601	ARK ROYAL	D834	PATHFINDER
D602	BULLDOG	D835	PEGASUS
D603	CONQUEST	D836	POWERFUL
D604	COSSACK	D837	RAMILLIES
D800	SIR BRIAN ROBERTSON	D838	RAPID
D801	VANGUARD	D839	RELENTLESS
D802	FORMIDABLE	D840	RESISTANCE
D803	ALBION	D841	ROEBUCK
D804	AVENGER	D842	ROYAL OAK
D805	BENBOW	D843	SHARPSHOOTER
D806	CAMBRIAN	D844	SPARTAN
D807	CARADOC	D845	SPRIGHTLY
D808	CENTAUR	D846	STEADFAST
D809	CHAMPION	D847	STRONGBOW
D810	COCKADE	D848	SULTAN
D811	DARING	D849	SUPERB
D812	THE ROYAL NAVAL 1859 RESERVE 1959	D850	SWIFT
D813	DIADEM	D851	TEMERAIRE
D814	DRAGON	D852	TENACIOUS
D815	DRUID	D853	THRUSTER
D816	ECLIPSE	D854	TIGER
D817	FOXHOUND	D855	TRIUMPH
D818	GLORY	D856	TROJAN
D819	GOLIATH	D857	UNDAUNTED
D820	GRENVILLE	D858	VALOROUS
D821	GREYHOUND	D859	VANQUISHER
D822	HERCULES	D860	VICTORIOUS
D823	HERMES	D861	VIGILANT
D824	HIGHFLYER	D862	VIKING
D825	INTREPID	D863	WARRIOR
D826	JUPITER	D864	ZAMBESI
D827	KELLY	D865	ZEALOUS
D828	MAGNIFICENT	D866	ZEBRA
D829	MAGPIE	D867	ZENITH
D830	MAJESTIC	D868	ZEPHYR
D831	MONARCH	D869	ZEST
D832	ONSLAUGHT	D870	ZULU

Note: Many of these locomotives had lost the 'D' prefix to their numbers by the time of withdrawal.

D802 *D.H. Cape*

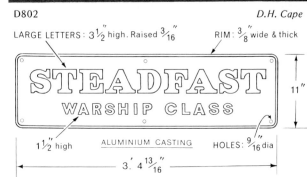

LARGE LETTERS : 3½″ high. Raised 3/16″   RIM : 3/8″ wide & thick

11″

1½″ high   ALUMINIUM CASTING   HOLES: 9/16″ dia

3′ 4 13/16″

No.70 (later No.45 048) THE ROYAL MARINES leaving Taunton on a North-West train. *C.L. Caddy*

'PEAK' CLASSES 44, 45 & 46

The first 10 locomotives, named after mountain peaks, make up the Class 44, introduced in 1959. From 1960, Class 45 appeared, and eventually 26 of the 127 were named. Then, from 1961, a total of 56 locomotives of Class 46 were built, only one of which has been named. All originally ran on the London Midland Region.

44 001	SCAFELL PIKE	44 006	WHERNSIDE
44 002	HELVELLYN	44 007	INGLEBOROUGH
44 003	SKIDDAW	44 008	PENYGHENT
44 004	GREAT GABLE	44 009	SNOWDON
44 005	CROSS FELL	44 010	TRYFAN

45 004 ROYAL IRISH FUSILIER*
45 006 HONOURABLE ARTILLERY COMPANY*
45 014 THE CHESHIRE REGIMENT*
45 022 LYTHAM ST. ANNES
45 023 THE ROYAL PIONEER CORPS*
45 039 THE MANCHESTER REGIMENT*
45 040 KING'S SHROPSHIRE LIGHT INFANTRY*
45 041 ROYAL TANK REGIMENT*
45 043 THE KING'S OWN
       ROYAL BORDER REGIMENT*
45 044 ROYAL INNISKILLING FUSILIER*
45 045 COLDSTREAM GUARDSMAN*
45 046 ROYAL FUSILIER*
45 048 THE ROYAL MARINES*
45 049 THE STAFFORDSHIRE REGIMENT
       (THE PRINCE OF WALES'S)*
45 055 ROYAL CORPS OF TRANSPORT*
45 059 ROYAL ENGINEER*
45 060 SHERWOOD FORESTER*
45 104 THE ROYAL WARWICKSHIRE FUSILIER*
45 111 GRENADIER GUARDSMAN*
45 112 THE ROYAL ARMY ORDNANCE CORPS*
45 118 THE ROYAL ARTILLERYMAN*
45 123 THE LANCASHIRE FUSILIER*
45 135 3RD CARABINIER*
45 137 THE BEDFORSHIRE AND HERTFORDSHIRE
       REGIMENT (T.A.)*
45 143 5TH ROYAL INNISKILLING
       DRAGOON GUARDS*
45 144 ROYAL SIGNALS*

46 026 LEICESTERSHIRE AND DERBYSHIRE
       YEOMANRY*

These locomotives carry a regimental crest above the nameplate.

No.44 004 *D.L. Percival*

No.45 137 *C.L. Caddy*

No.45 004, one of the few with a surround to the nameplate. *D.L. Percival*

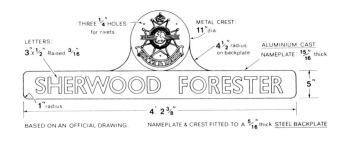

THREE 1/4" HOLES for rivets
METAL CREST: 11" dia.
LETTERS: 3"x1/2" Raised 3/16
4 1/2" radius on backplate
ALUMINIUM CAST NAMEPLATE: 15/16" thick
SHERWOOD FORESTER
5"
1"radius
4' 2 3/8"
BASED ON AN OFFICIAL DRAWING.   NAMEPLATE & CREST FITTED TO A 5/16" thick STEEL BACKPLATE

No.D1000, first of the class, at Cardiff.   *D.L. Percival*

No.D1006   *D.H. Cape*

No.D1062   *L.M. Hobdey*

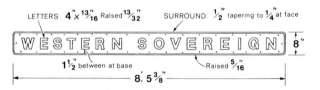
LETTERS: 4"× $\frac{13}{16}$" Raised $\frac{13}{32}$"   SURROUND: $\frac{1}{2}$" tapering to $\frac{1}{4}$" at face

WESTERN SOVEREIGN   8"

$1\frac{1}{2}$" between at base   Raised $\frac{5}{16}$"

8' 5$\frac{3}{8}$"

CLASS 53

Also introduced in 1961, was an experimental high-powered locomotive, which has seen service on several regions, particularly the Western lines.

Left: C. Field

'WESTERN' CLASS 52

This class, introduced in 1961, was built solely for the Western Region and all 74 locomotives were named. The nameplates were fabricated; the aluminium letters and beading being fixed to a steel backplate.

D1000	WESTERN ENTERPRISE	D1037	WESTERN EMPRESS
D1001	WESTERN PATHFINDER	D1038	WESTERN SOVEREIGN
D1002	WESTERN EXPLORER	D1039	WESTERN KING
D1003	WESTERN PIONEER	D1040	WESTERN QUEEN
D1004	WESTERN CRUSADER	D1041	WESTERN PRINCE
D1005	WESTERN VENTURER	D1042	WESTERN PRINCESS
D1006	WESTERN STALWART	D1043	WESTERN DUKE
D1007	WESTERN TALISMAN	D1044	WESTERN DUCHESS
D1008	WESTERN HARRIER	D1045	WESTERN VISCOUNT
D1009	WESTERN INVADER	D1046	WESTERN MARQUIS
D1010	WESTERN CAMPAIGNER	D1047	WESTERN LORD
D1011	WESTERN THUNDERER	D1048	WESTERN LADY
D1012	WESTERN FIREBRAND	D1049	WESTERN MONARCH
D1013	WESTERN RANGER	D1050	WESTERN RULER
D1014	WESTERN LEVIATHAN	D1051	WESTERN AMBASSADOR
D1015	WESTERN CHAMPION	D1052	WESTERN VICEROY
D1016	WESTERN GLADIATOR	D1053	WESTERN PATRIARCH
D1017	WESTERN WARRIOR	D1054	WESTERN GOVERNOR
D1018	WESTERN BUCCANEER	D1055	WESTERN ADVOCATE
D1019	WESTERN CHALLENGER	D1056	WESTERN SULTAN
D1020	WESTERN HERO	D1057	WESTERN CHIEFTAIN
D1021	WESTERN CAVALIER	D1058	WESTERN NOBLEMAN
D1022	WESTERN SENTINEL	D1059	WESTERN EMPIRE
D1023	WESTERN FUSILIER	D1060	WESTERN DOMINION
D1024	WESTERN HUNTSMAN	D1061	WESTERN ENVOY
D1025	WESTERN GUARDSMAN	D1062	WESTERN COURIER
D1026	WESTERN CENTURION	D1063	WESTERN MONITOR
D1027	WESTERN LANCER	D1064	WESTERN REGENT
D1028	WESTERN HUSSAR	D1065	WESTERN CONSORT
D1029	WESTERN LEGIONAIRE/	D1066	WESTERN PREFECT
D1029	WESTERN LEGIONNAIRE	D1067	WESTERN DRUID
D1030	WESTERN MUSKETEER	D1068	WESTERN RELIANCE
D1031	WESTERN RIFLEMAN	D1069	WESTERN VANGUARD
D1032	WESTERN MARKSMAN	D1070	WESTERN GAUNTLET
D1033	WESTERN TROOPER	D1071	WESTERN RENOWN
D1034	WESTERN DRAGOON	D1072	WESTERN GLORY
D1035	WESTERN YEOMAN	D1073	WESTERN BULWARK
D1036	WESTERN EMPEROR		

Note: Although the 'D' prefix to the numbers is not now officially used, it is quoted above as these locomotives have numberplates which are not being altered.

FALCON, as built with original number before being taken into B.R. stock.   *British Rail*

1200 FALCON

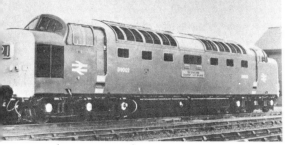

No.D9002 (later No.55 002)   *British Rail*

'DELTIC' CLASS 55

Introduced in 1961 for work on the Eastern and Scottish Regions, all 22 of the class are named.

55 001	ST. PADDY
55 002	THE KING'S OWN YORKSHIRE LIGHT INFANTRY
55 003	MELD
55 004	QUEEN'S OWN HIGHLANDER*
55 005	THE PRINCE OF WALES'S OWN REGIMENT OF YORKSHIRE
55 006	THE FIFE & FORFAR YEOMANRY*
55 007	PINZA
55 008	THE GREEN HOWARDS*
55 009	ALYCIDON
55 010	THE KING'S OWN SCOTTISH BORDERER*
55 011	THE ROYAL NORTHUMBERLAND FUSILIERS
55 012	CREPELLO
55 013	THE BLACK WATCH*
55 014	THE DUKE OF WELLINGTON'S REGIMENT*
55 015	TULYAR
55 016	GORDON HIGHLANDER*
55 017	THE DURHAM LIGHT INFANTRY
55 018	BALLYMOSS
55 019	ROYAL HIGHLAND FUSILIER*
55 020	NIMBUS
55 021	ARGYLL & SUTHERLAND HIGHLANDER*
55 022	ROYAL SCOTS GREY*

*At some time during service these locomotives carried a regimental crest.

No.55 002   *D.L. Percival*

No.55 022   *D.L. Percival*

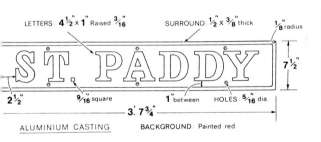

LETTERS **4½" × 1"** Raised **3/16"**   SURROUND **½" × 3/8" thick**   **1/8" radius**

7½"

2½"   **9/16" square**   **1" between**   HOLES **5/16" dia.**

3' 7¾"

ALUMINIUM CASTING   BACKGROUND : Painted red.

Above: No.55 007   *British Rail*

Below: No.55 006   *D.L. Percival*

CLASS 47

Built from 1962 and allocated to all Regions except the Southern, there are over 500 in this class, and the 17 named locomotives are amongst those worked by the Western Region.

Right: No.1662 (later No.47 484) at Weymouth Station, March, 1973.   *C.L. Caddy*

47 076 CITY OF TRURO
47 077 NORTH STAR
47 078 SIR DANIEL GOOCH
47 079 GEORGE JACKSON CHURCHWARD
47 080 **TITAN**
47 081 **ODIN**
47 082 **ATLAS**
47 083 **ORION**
47 085 **MAMMOTH**
47 086 **COLOSSUS**
47 087 **CYCLOPS**
47 088 **SAMSON**
47 089 **AMAZON**
47 090 **VULCAN**
47 091 **THOR***
47 484 ISAMBARD KINGDOM BRUNEL
47 538 **PYTHON**

No.47 484. One of the long nameplates which was fabricated on similar lines to the 'Western' Class 52 plates. The others with **SERIF** lettering were cast in aluminium as with the 'Warship' Classes 42 & 43.   *C.L. Caddy*

This name was previously carried by No.D1671 which was scrapped in 1966.

No. 47 079, longest plate in the class; it measures 12ft. 7in. long with 4in. high letters.   *D.L. Percival*

No. 47 081, shortest in the class; measuring 1ft. 11 1/16 in. long with 3½in. high letters.   *D.L. Percival*

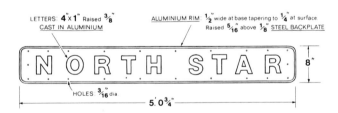

LETTERS: 4"x1" Raised 3/8" CAST IN ALUMINIUM
ALUMINIUM RIM: ½" wide at base tapering to ¼" at surface. Raised 5/16" above 1/8" STEEL BACKPLATE
8"
HOLES: 3/16" dia
5' 0¾"

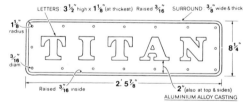

LETTERS 3½" high x 1 1/8" (at thickest) Raised 3/16"
SURROUND 3/8" wide & thick
1 1/8" radius
3/16" diam
8¼"
Raised 3/16" inside
2' 5 7/8"
2" (also at top & sides) ALUMINIUM ALLOY CASTING

Notes: The above are based on official drawings and some variation may be found on the actual nameplates. Although the Western Region adopted black for the background colour of their nameplates, red is used at times, as with the other regions.

No.47 090.   *D.L. Percival*

Right: Mr. Sidney Greene, General Secretary of the N.U.R. names one of the class at Paddington Station in 1966.